SURREAL and Landscape

Art Reflections

VOL 4

L F Peterson Ph.D.
Peterson Art Gallery
Volume 3
Copyright © 2019

Welcome to the fourth edition of my creative art series. As a cognitive psychologist, I am aware of the contributions of gestalt to the field of art creation and interpretation. Art and psychology encourage creative, novel synthesis. Perceptions are a flux of continually moving conscious and unconscious cognitions forming Multi Factorial Apperceptions. Artists capture subjective experience and observers form new experiences. The greater the ambiguity, the greater the opportunity for aesthetic growth and cognitive change. My art is both an expression of creativity and a mechanism for ambiguity to value-maximize opportunities for interaction and novel interpretation.

Where scientists seek to narrow interpretation, artists seek to employ the Look, See, and Think approach maximize interpretations of their work. Gestalt psychology illustrates how minds interpret similarity, proximity, symmetry, and figure ground to form order out of chaos. Color, shape, distance and density stimulate memories and complex ideas. Ambiguity demands new perspectives until Eureka, or cognitive consistency is achieved.

I employ a small brush under magnification to create my art renderings. I trust my paintings will stimulate new emotional and intellectual awareness and understanding. I will be publishing over 1200 paintings in the near future and trust you will follow my creative efforts through the various volumes.

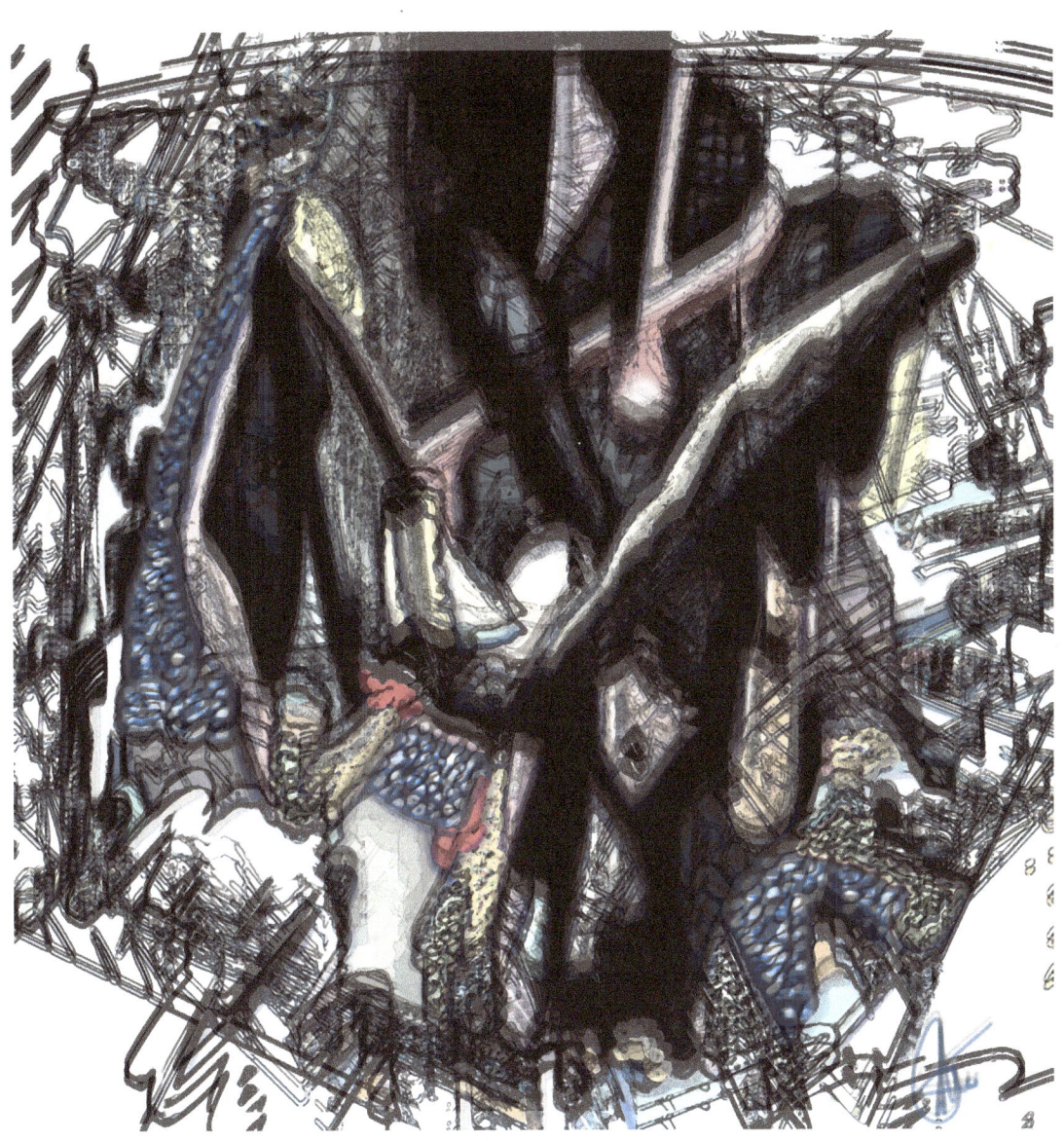

SMORGASMICSPECTATOR

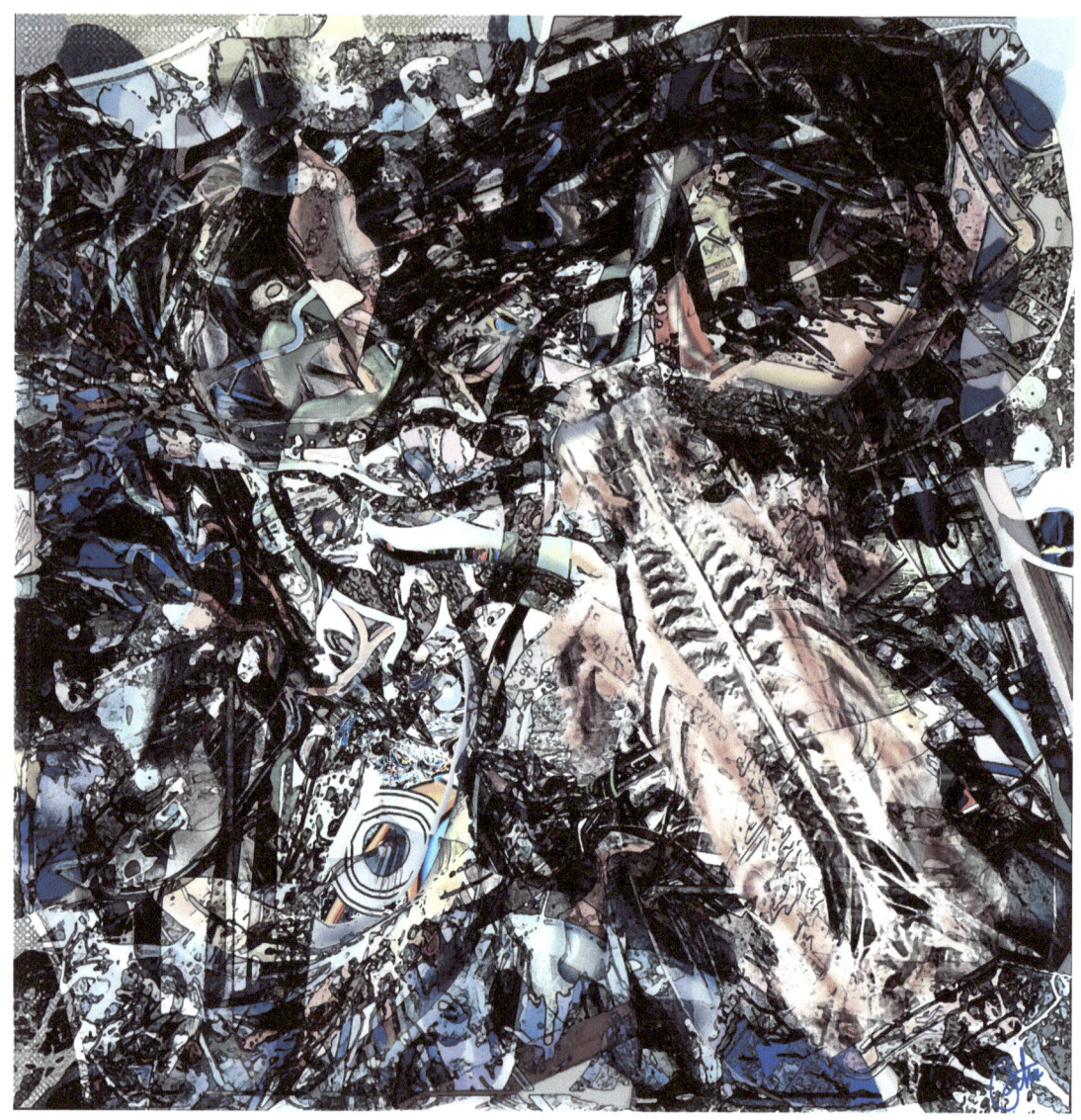

SPINAL
TAP

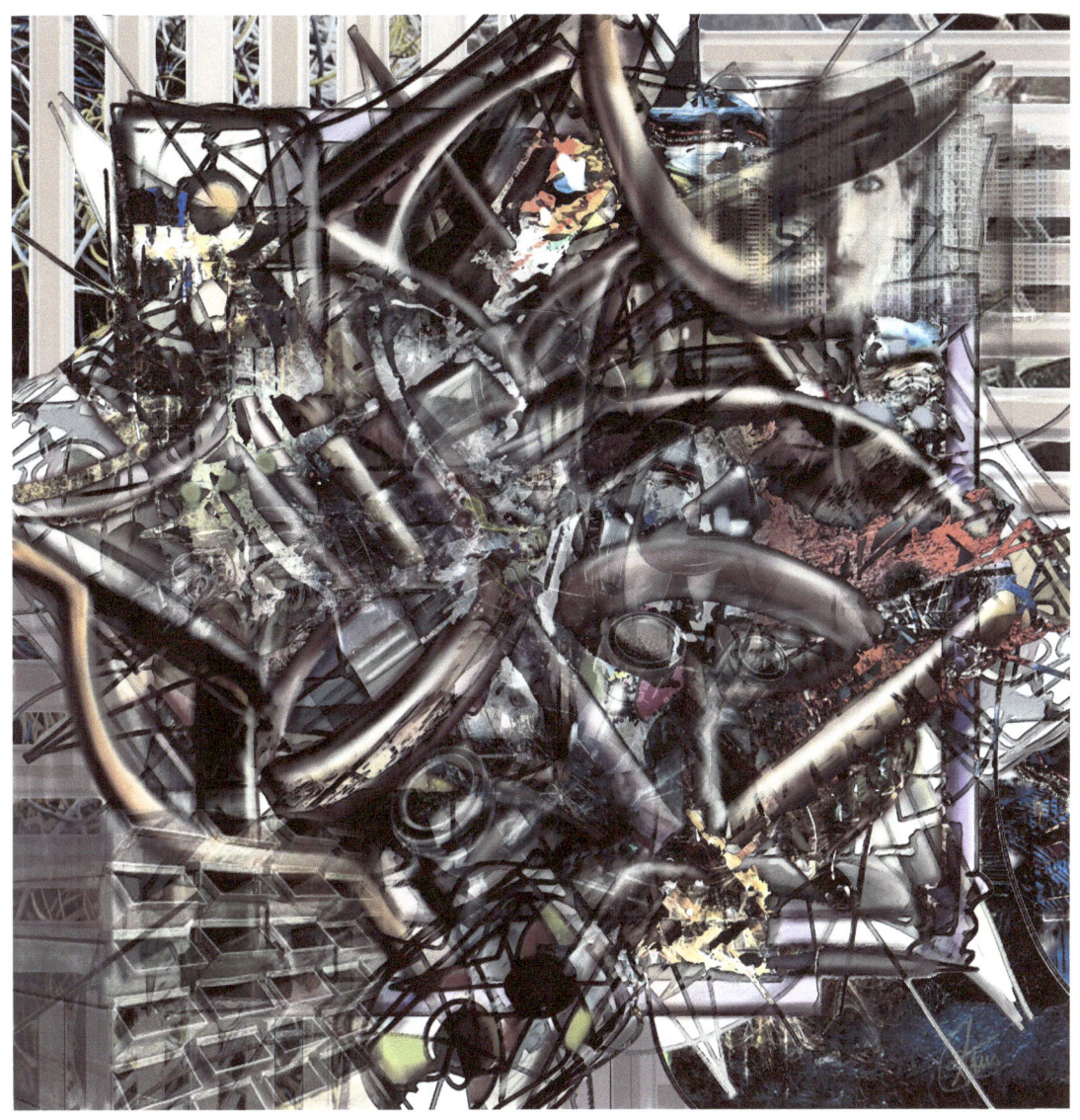

SPUR
STORAGE

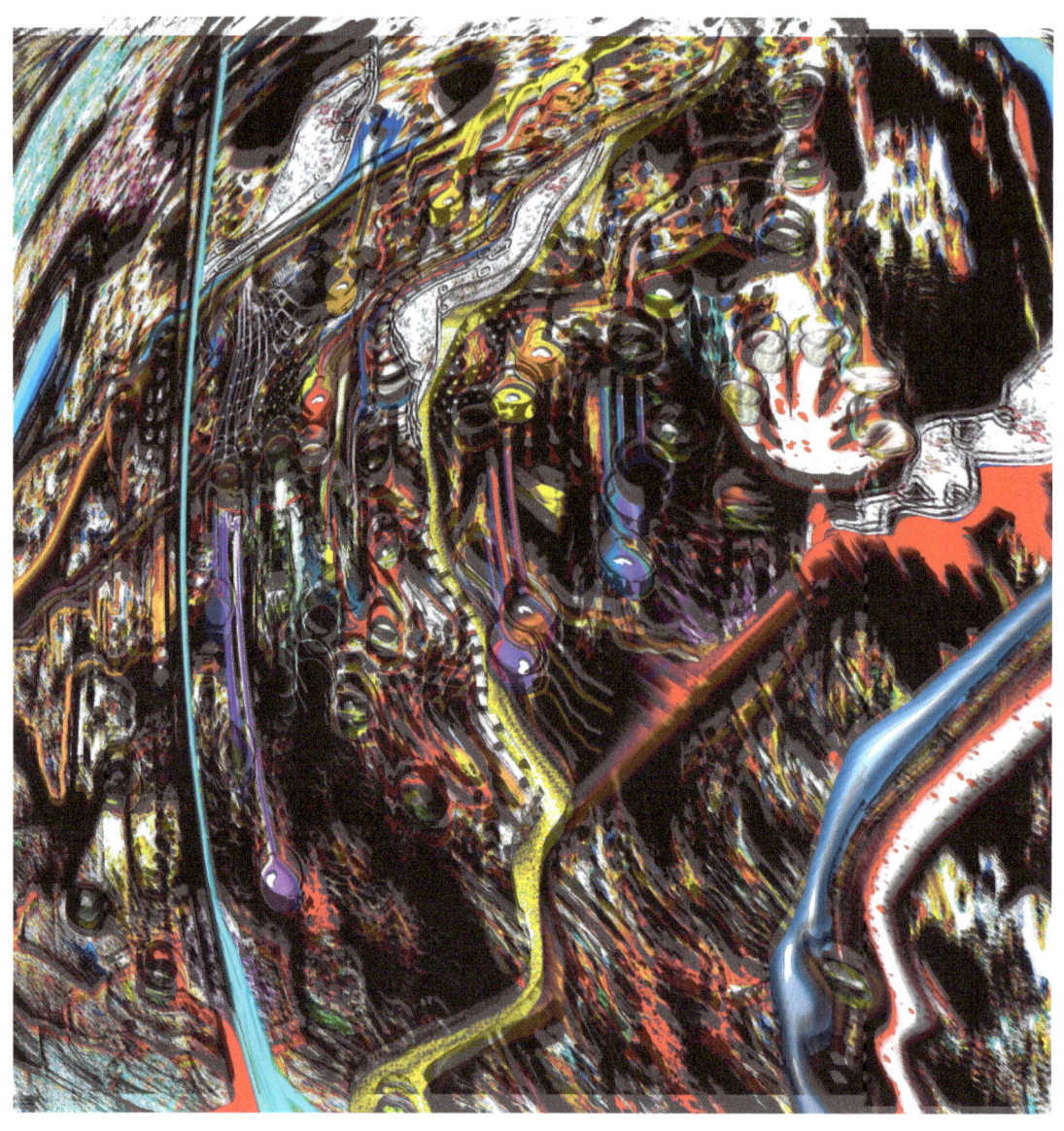

STEADFAST

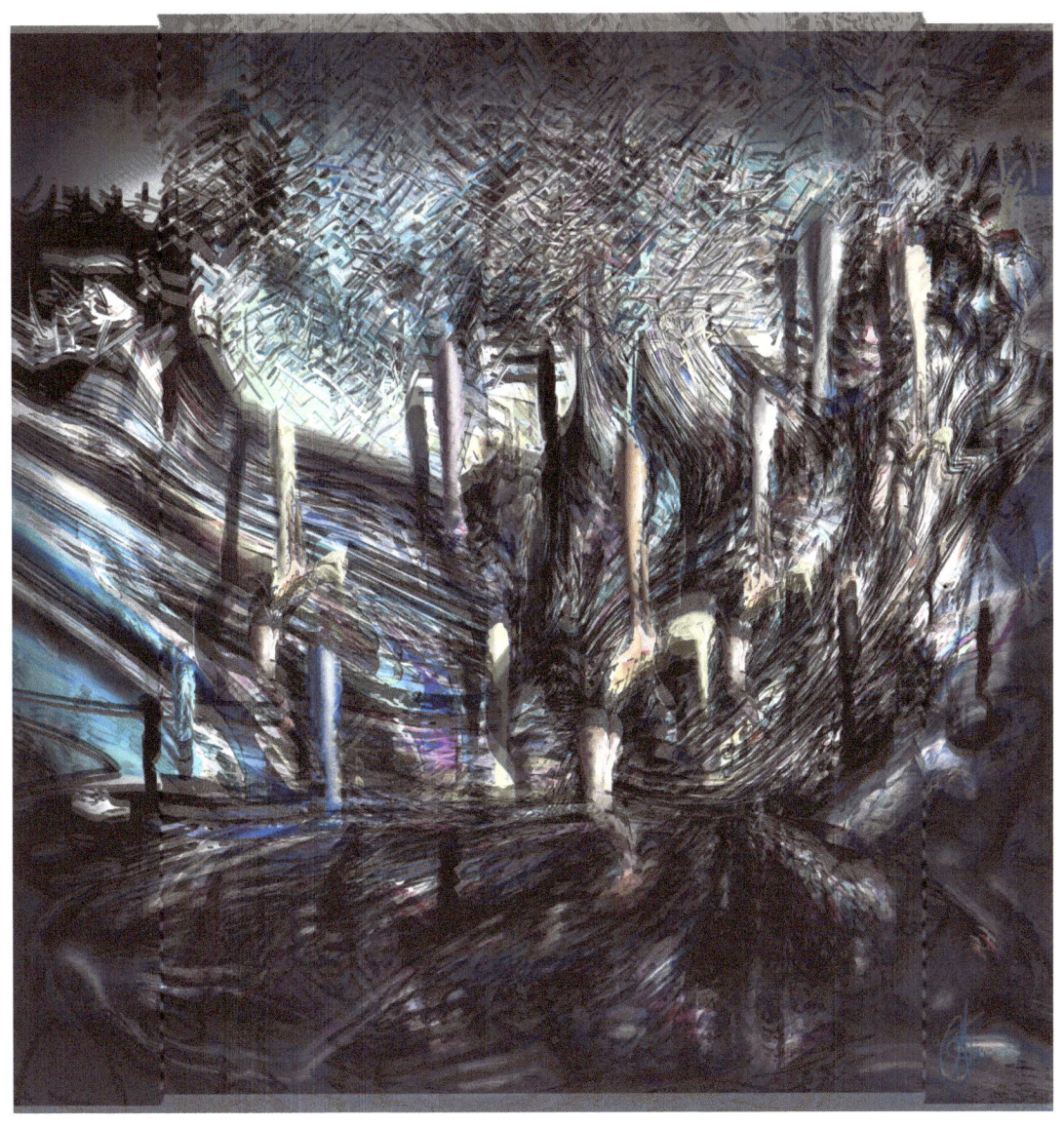

STEBLOTITES

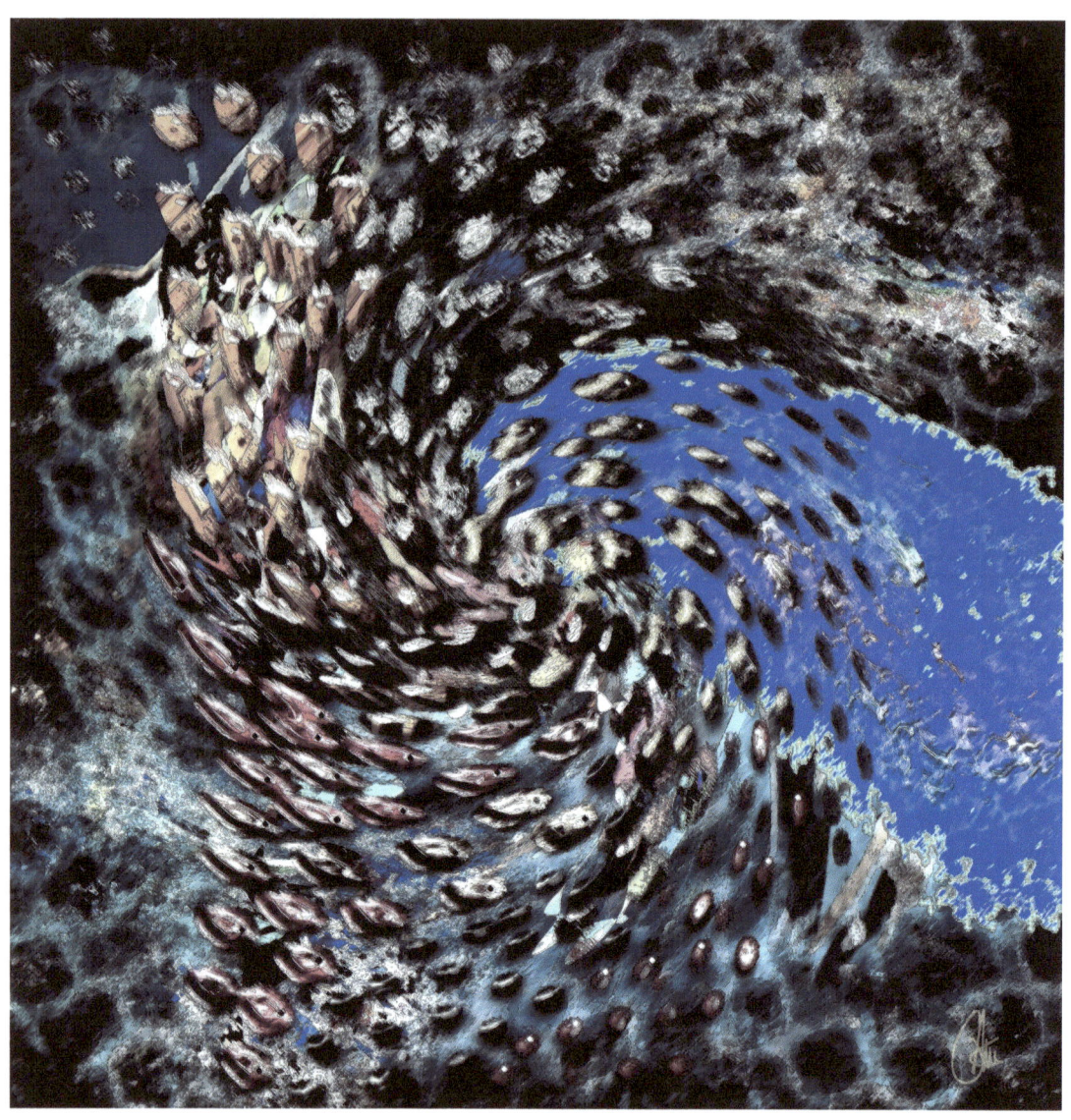

STRUCTURED
EXPERIENCES

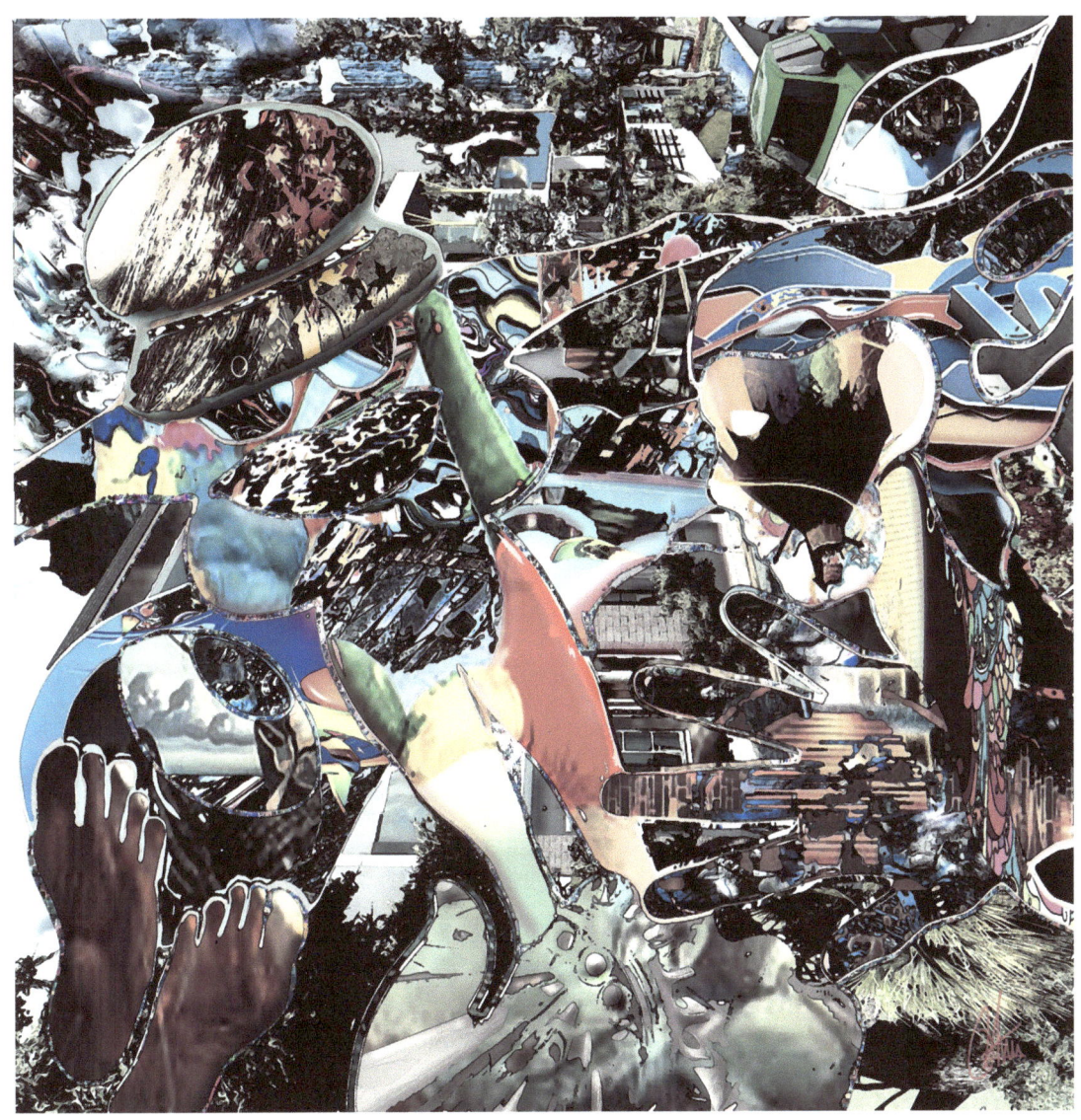

SUBURB
SUTRA

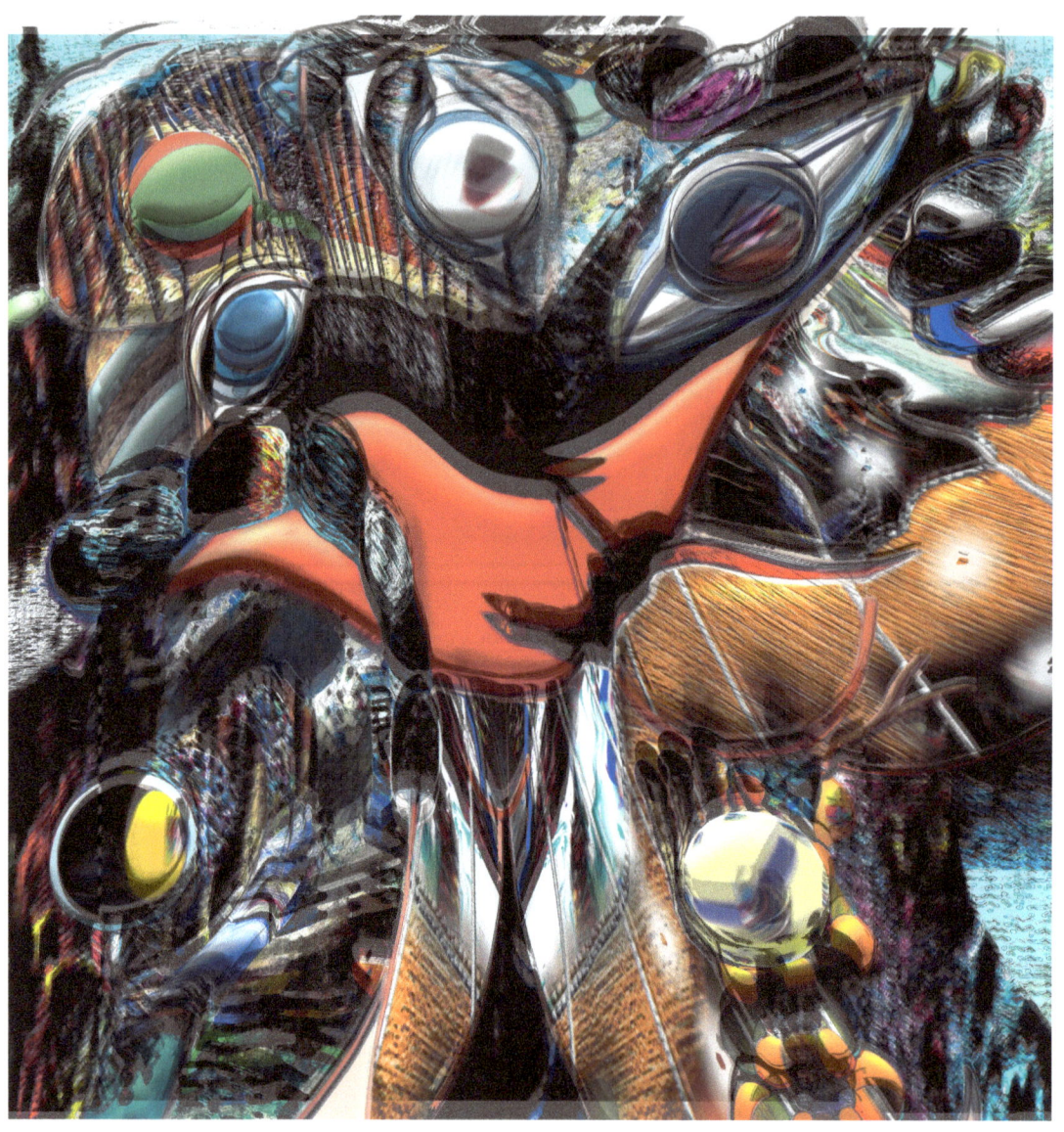

SWINGER
RED

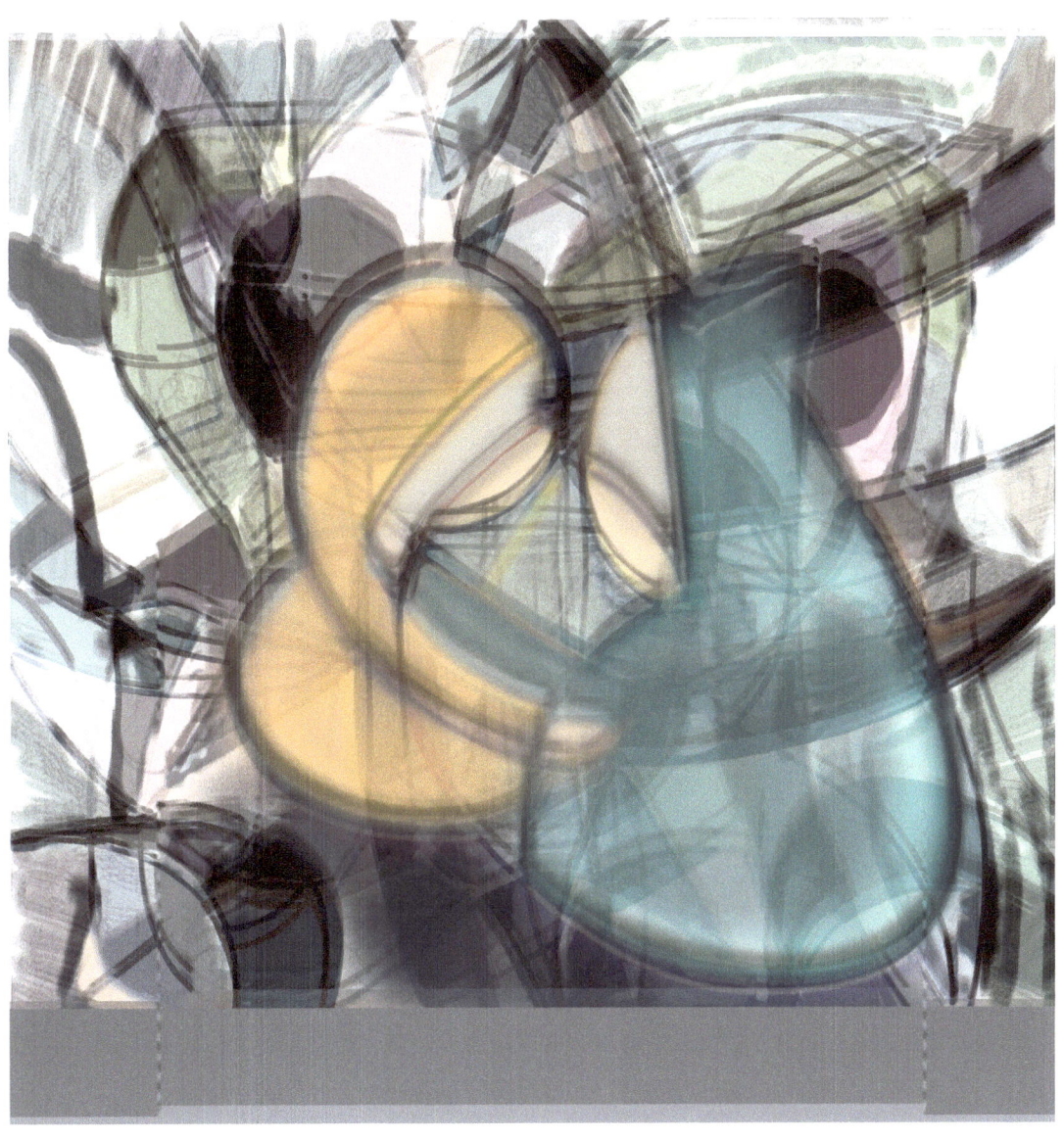

SYMPATHY

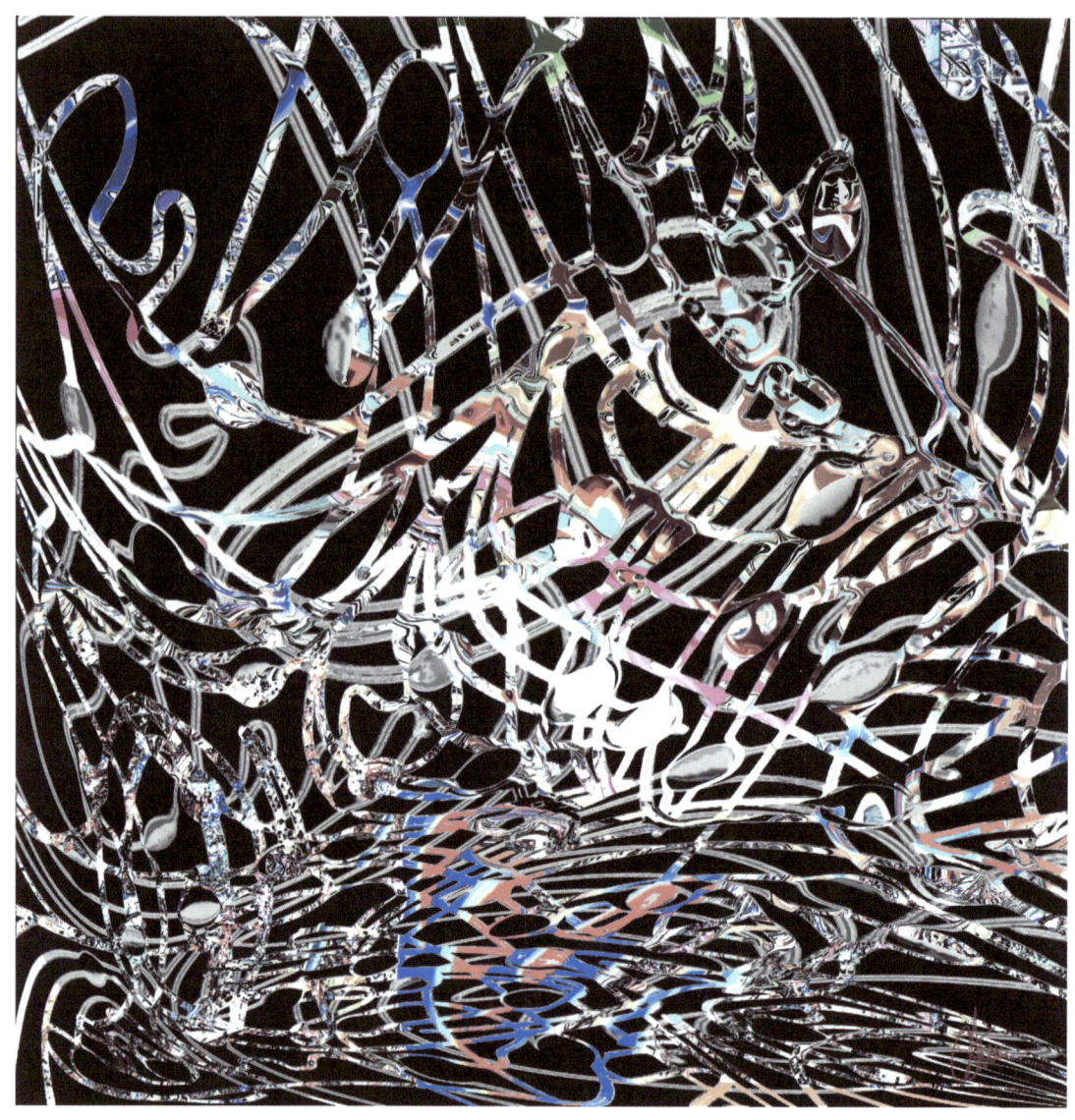

TAFFY
MADRIS

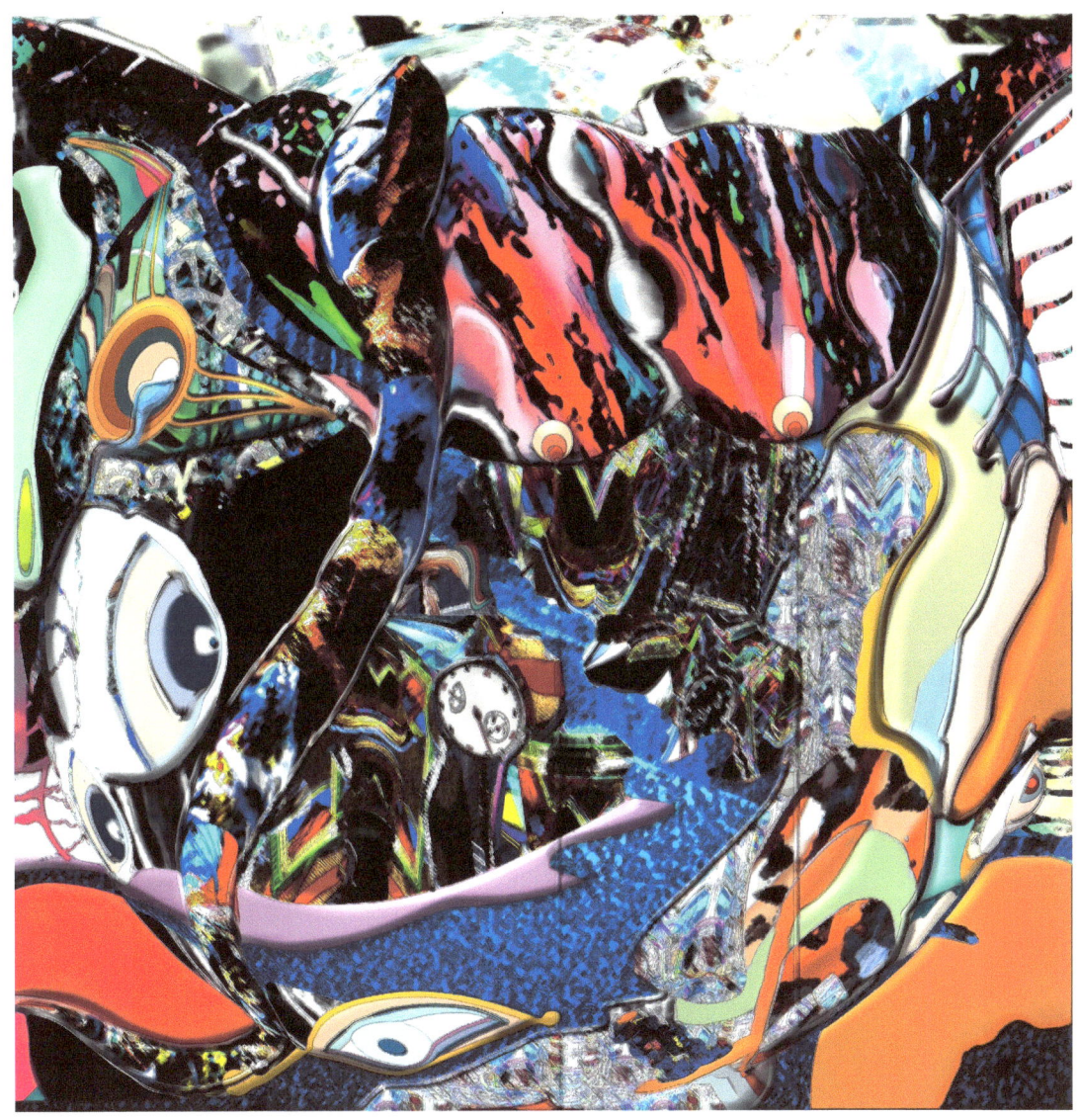

TESTONES

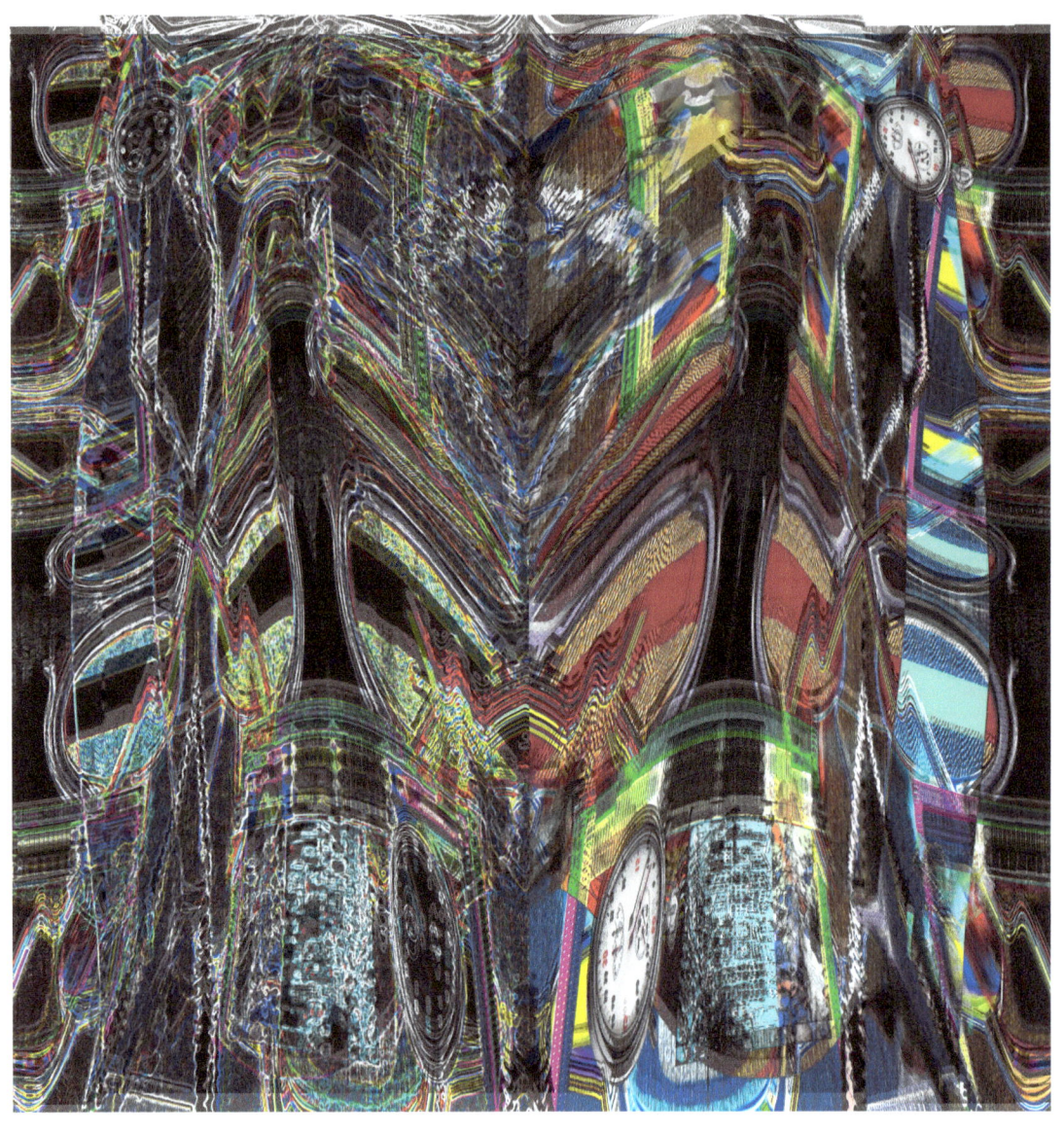

TEMPORESTRA

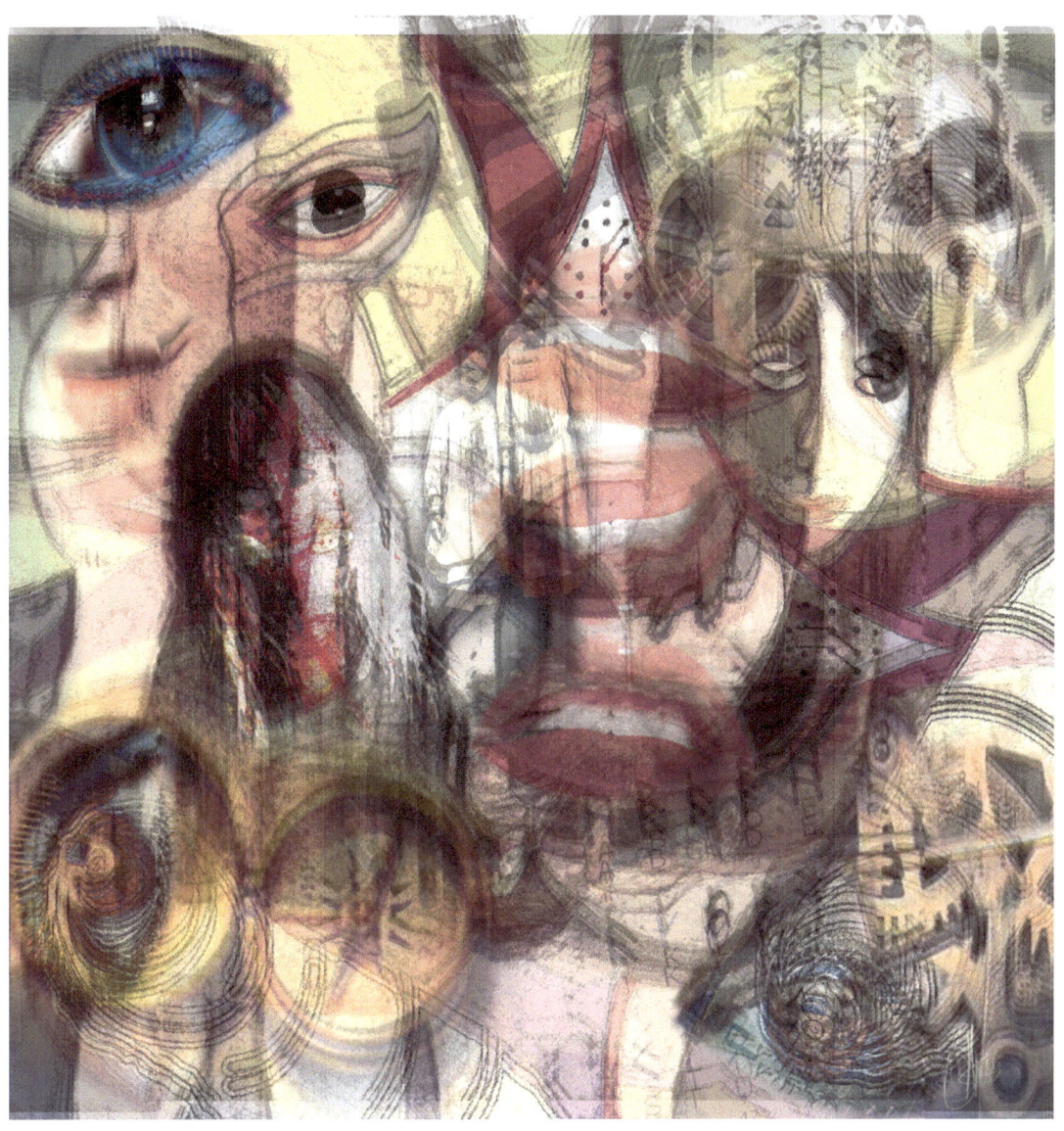

THE COUNSELOR

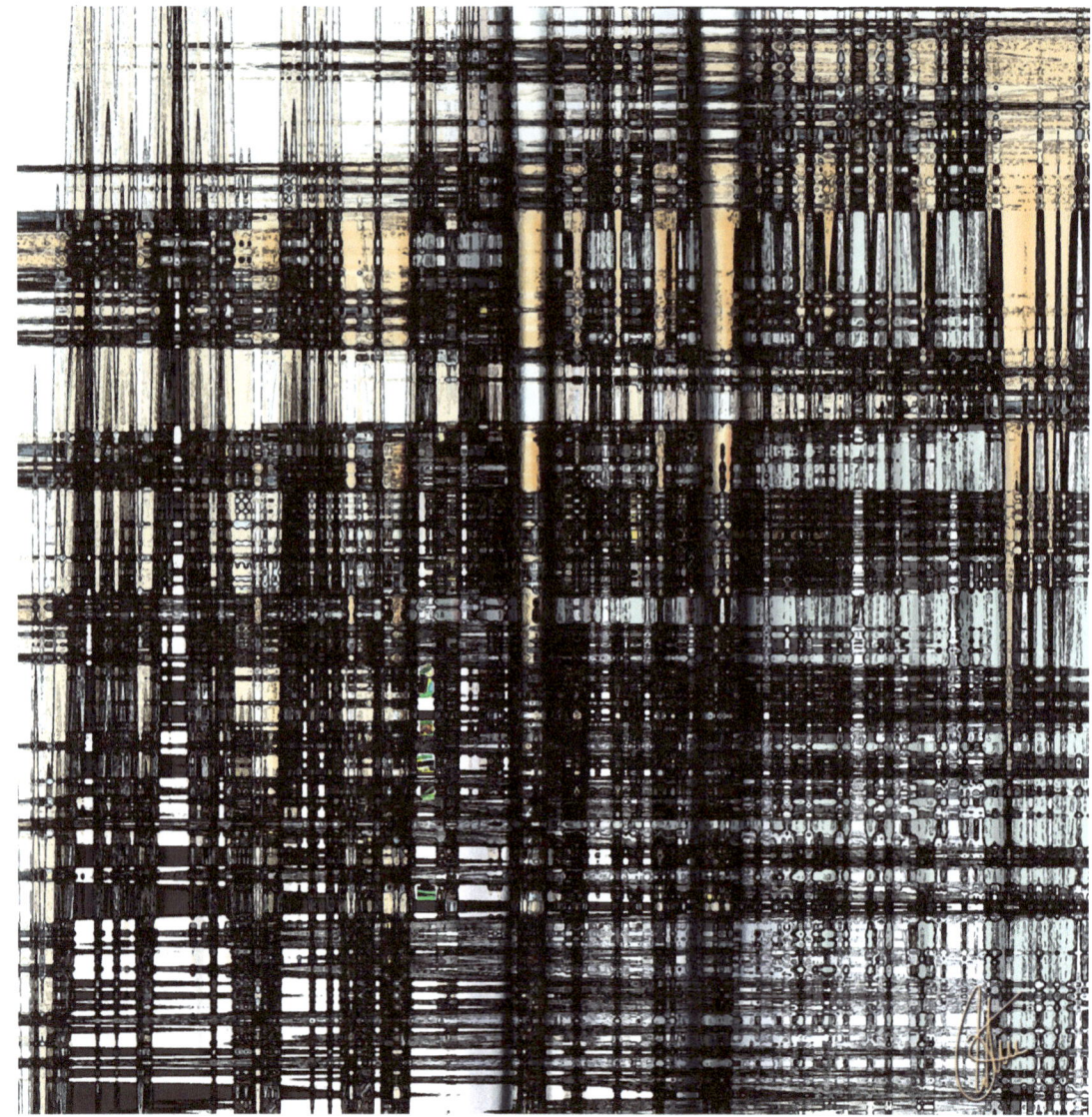

TOTE
SACK

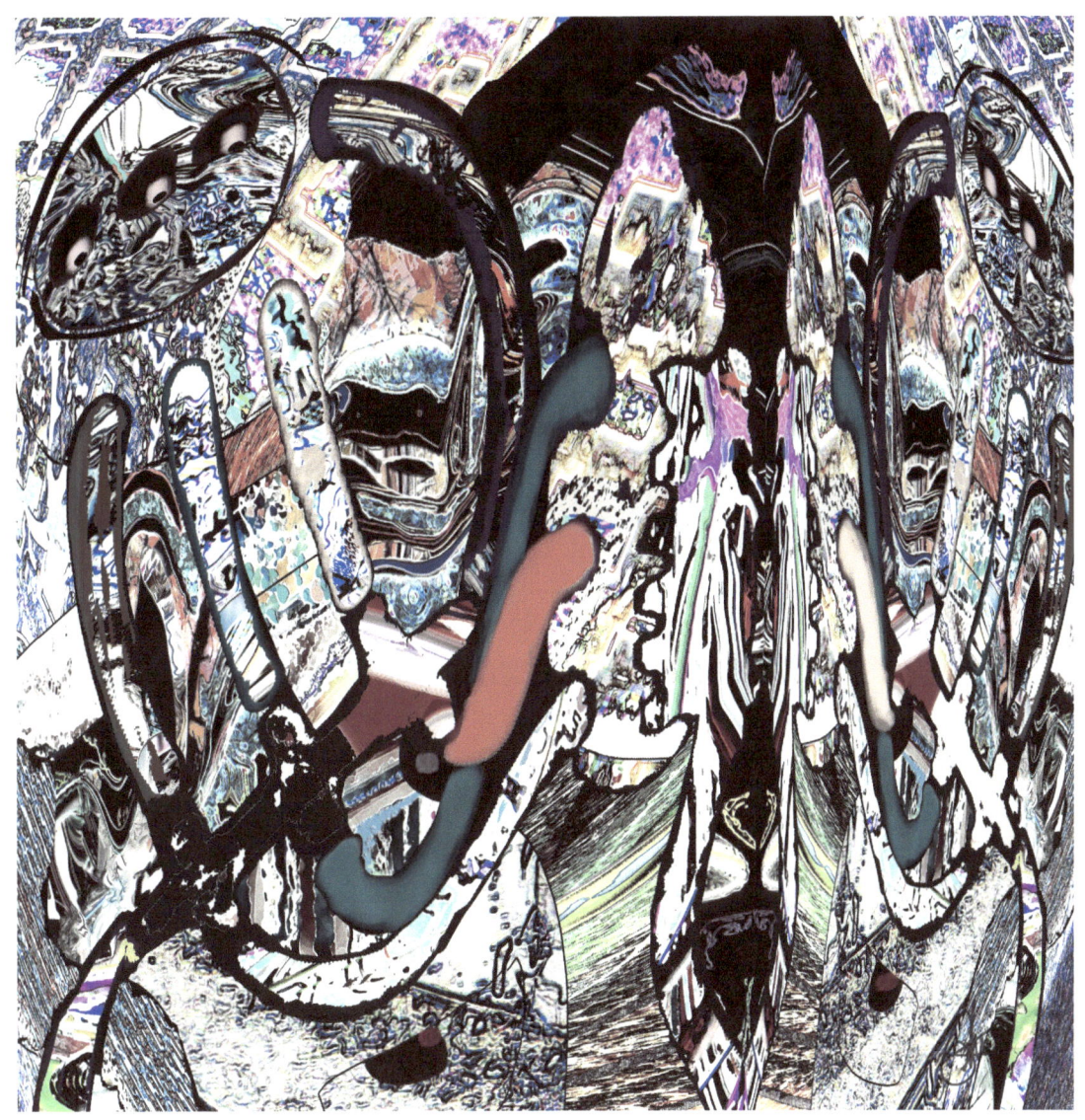

TOTEM

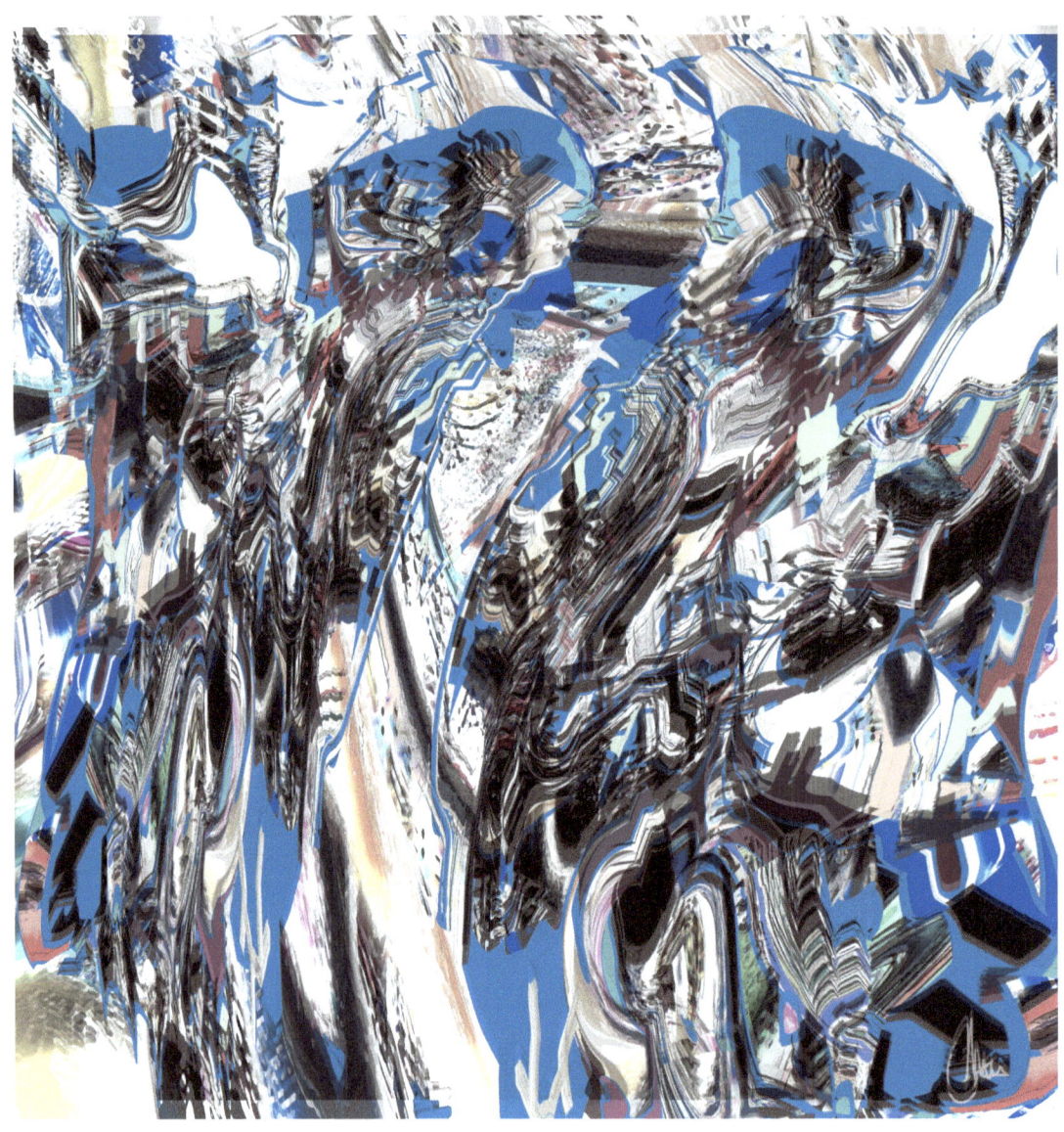

TRIBAL
GATHERING

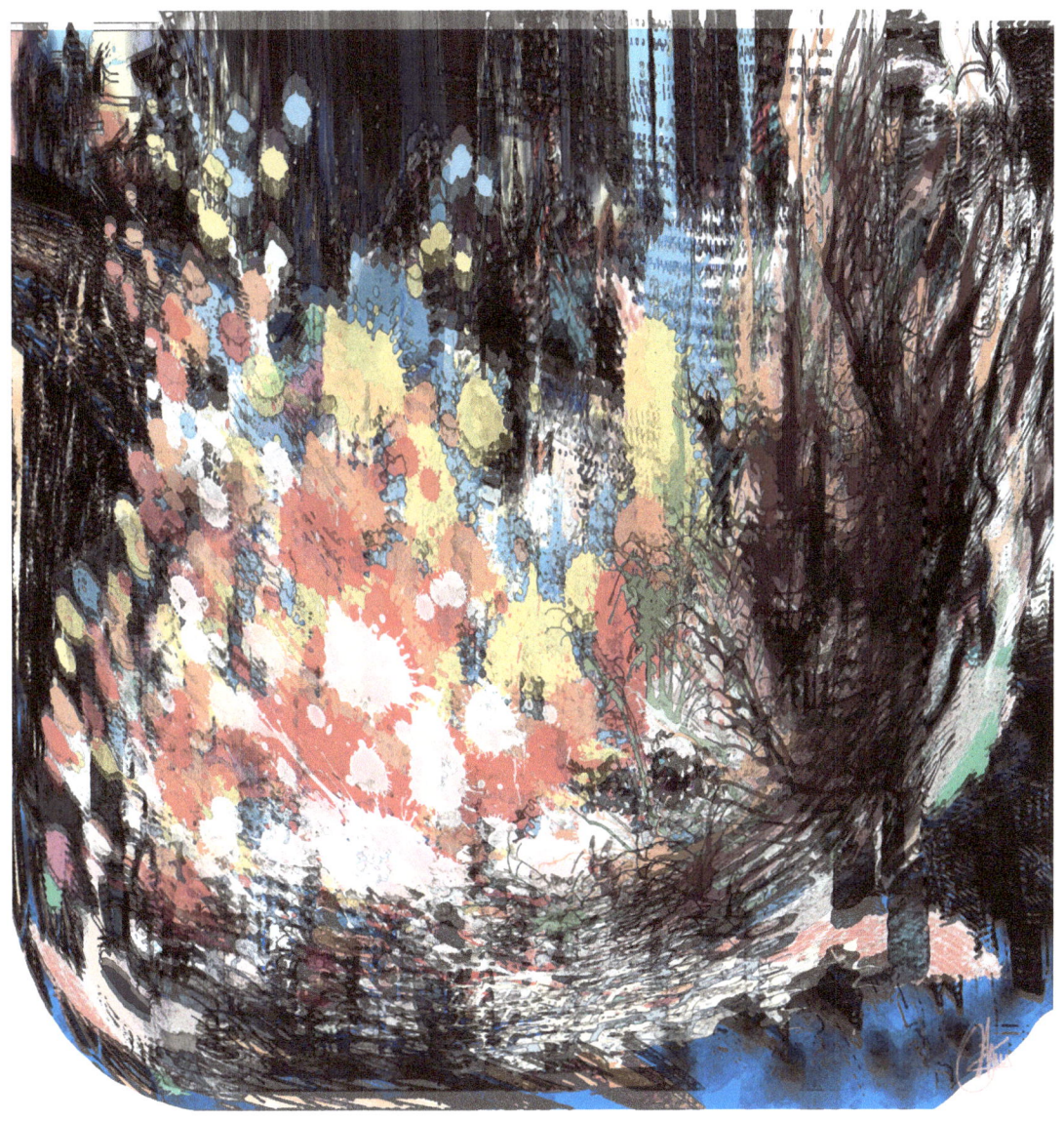

TRICITY

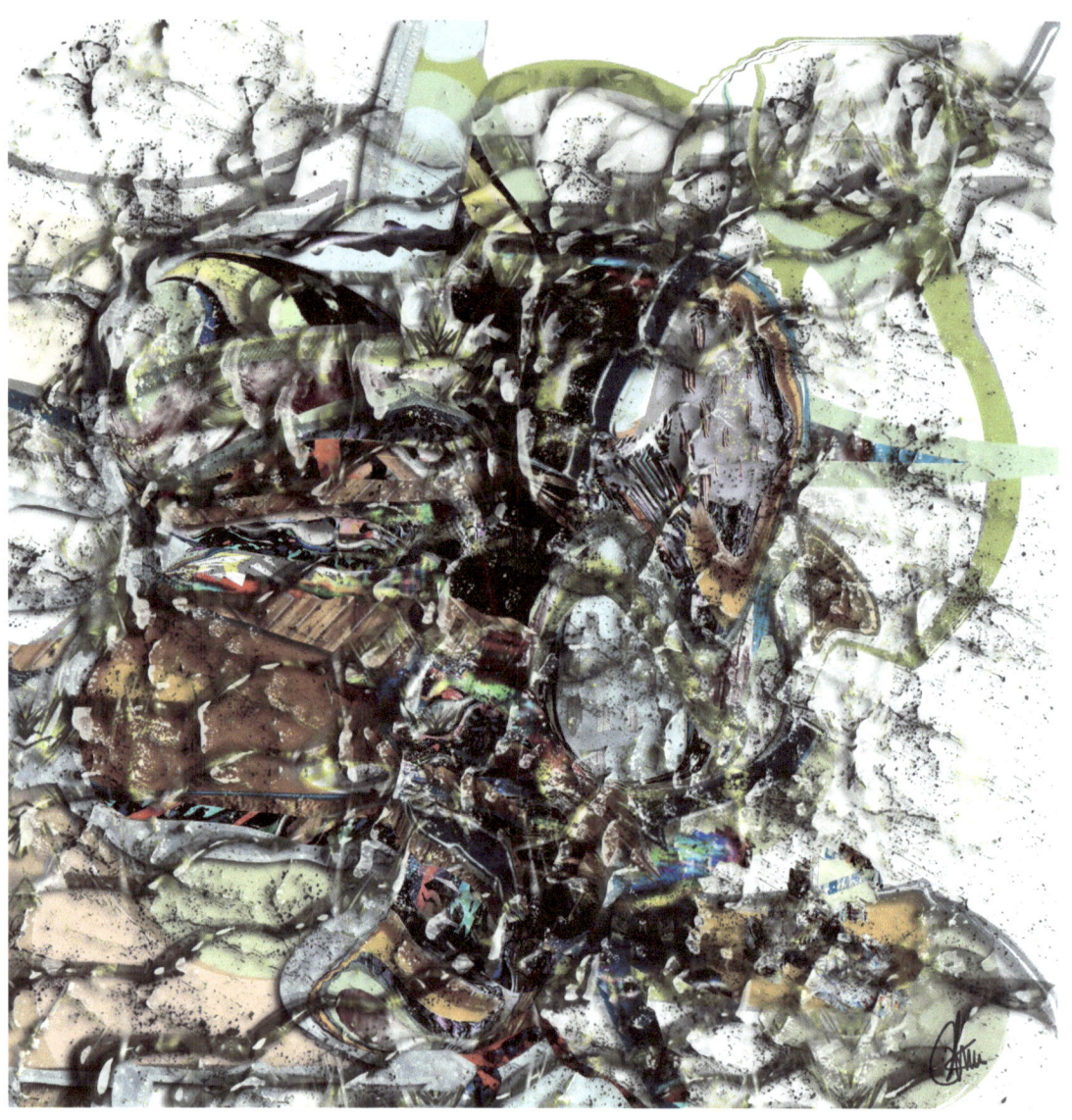

VISAGIO

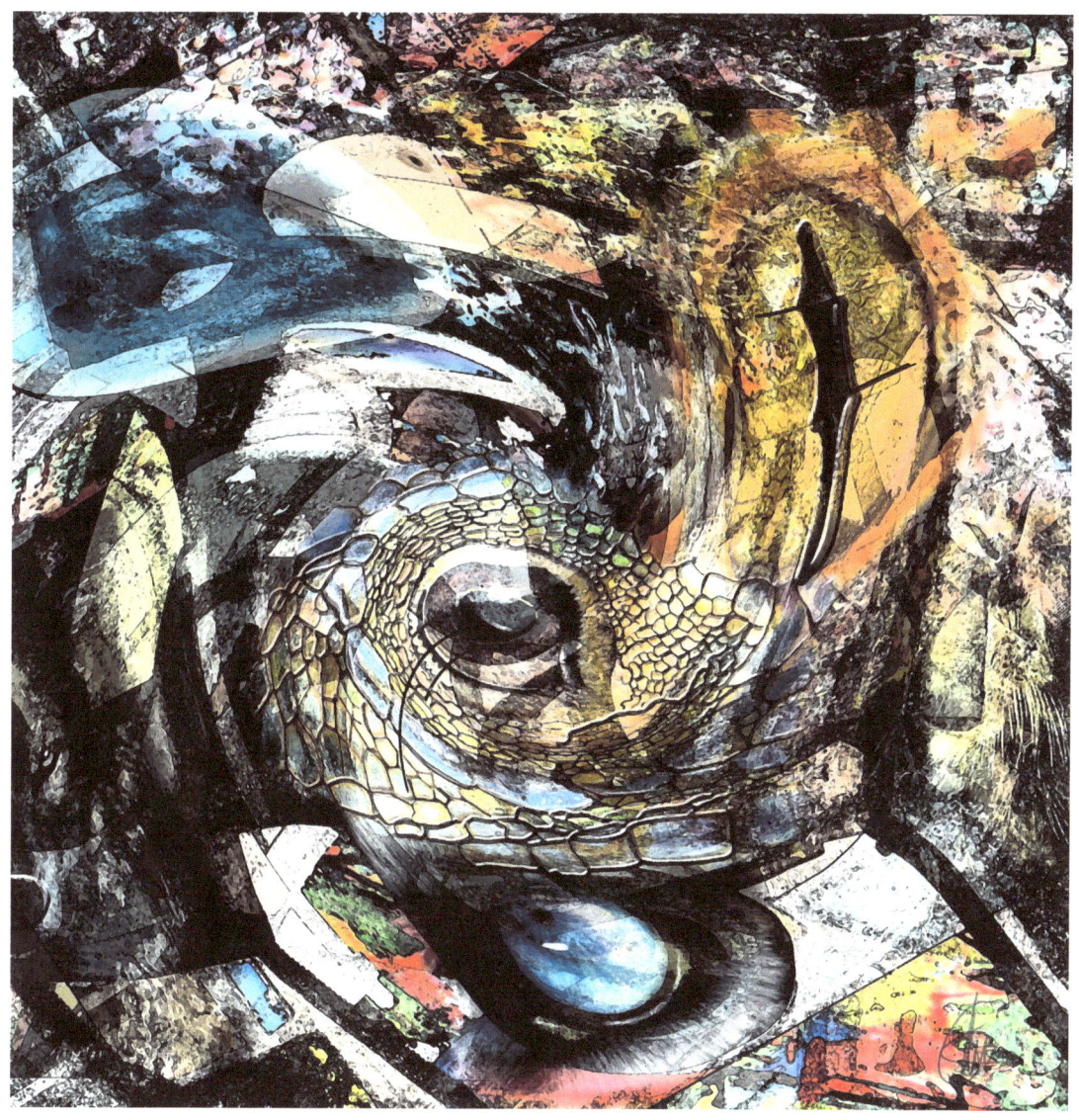

VISION
QUEST

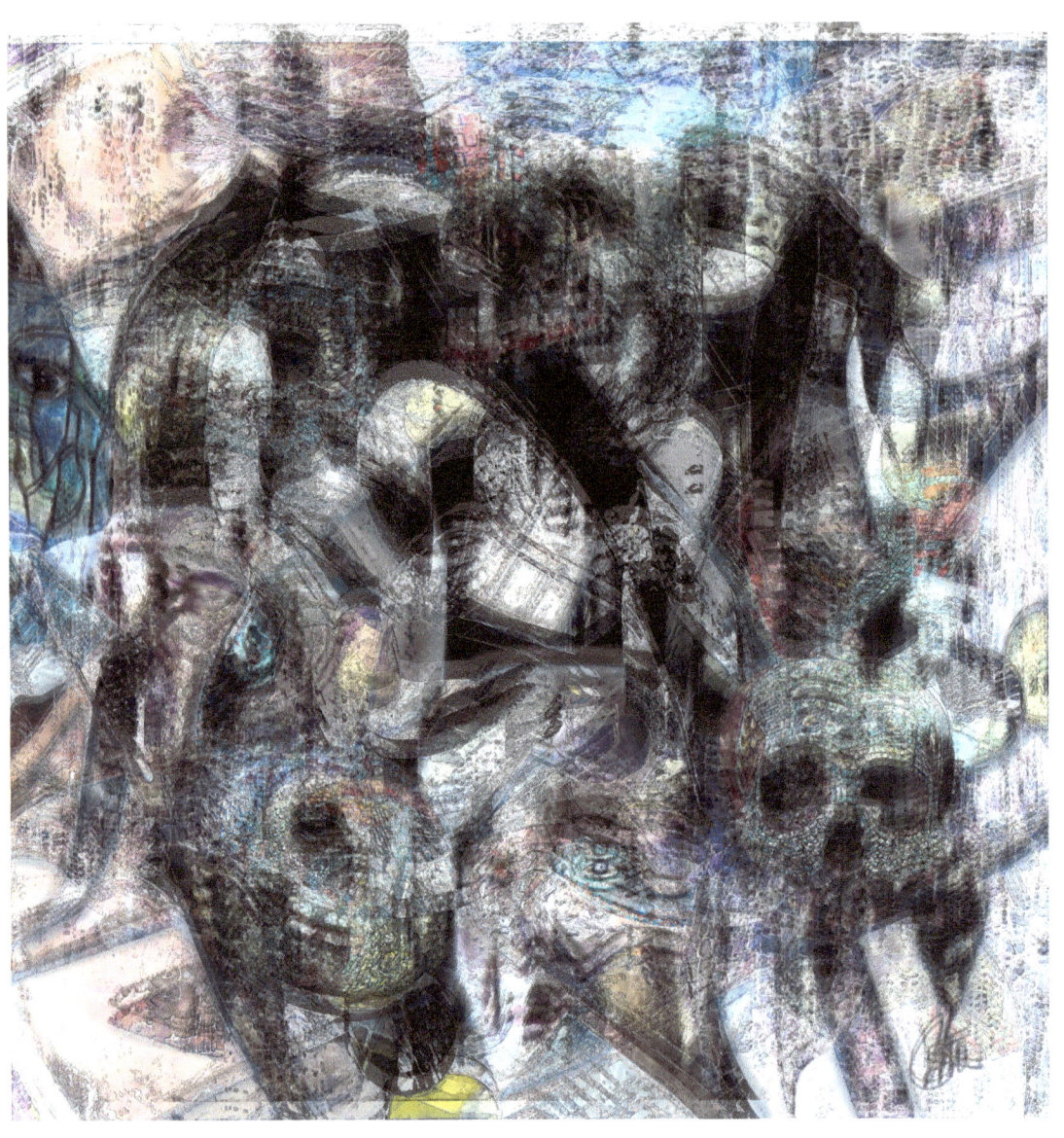

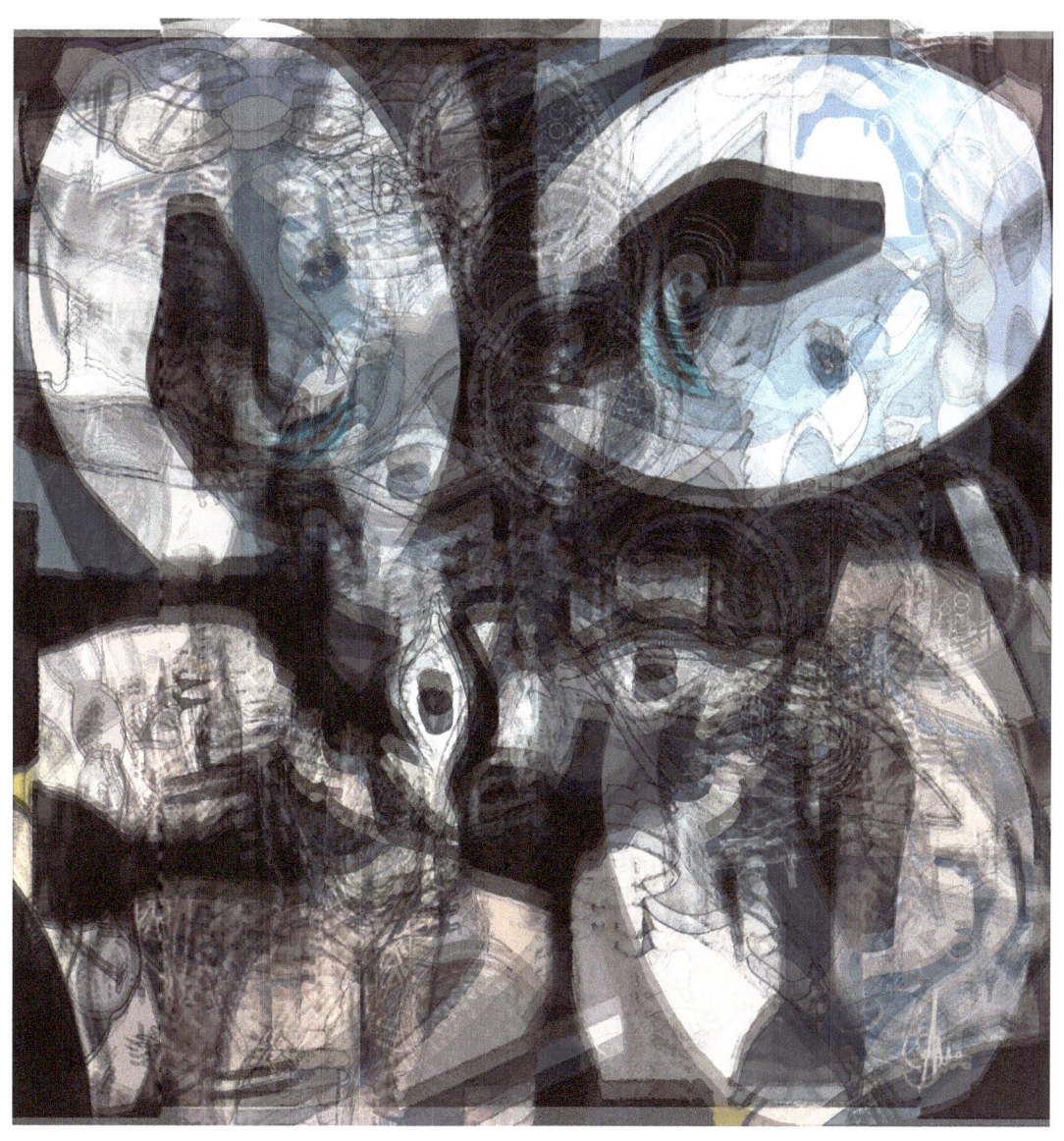

WHALEWATCH

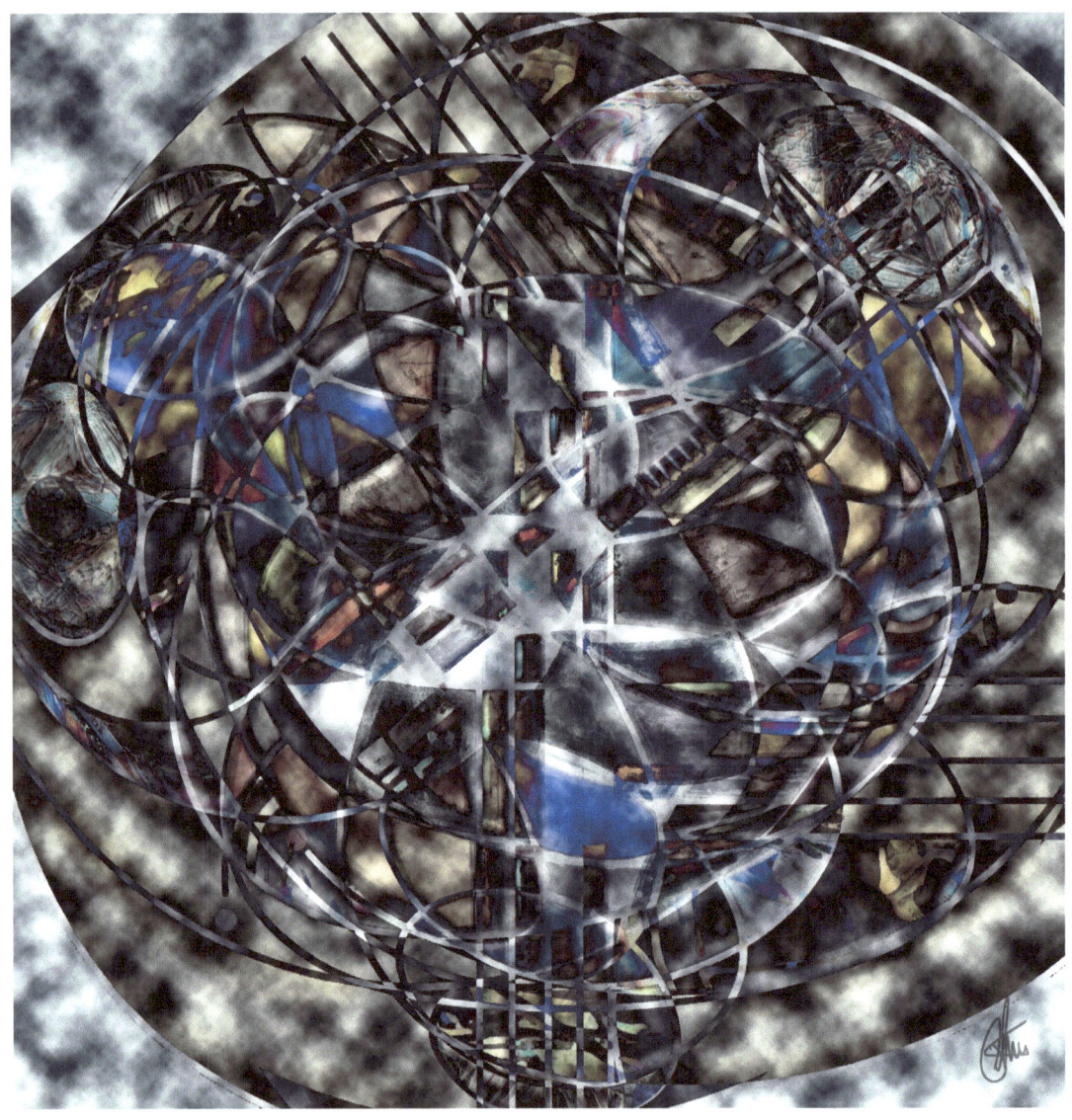

WICKEN

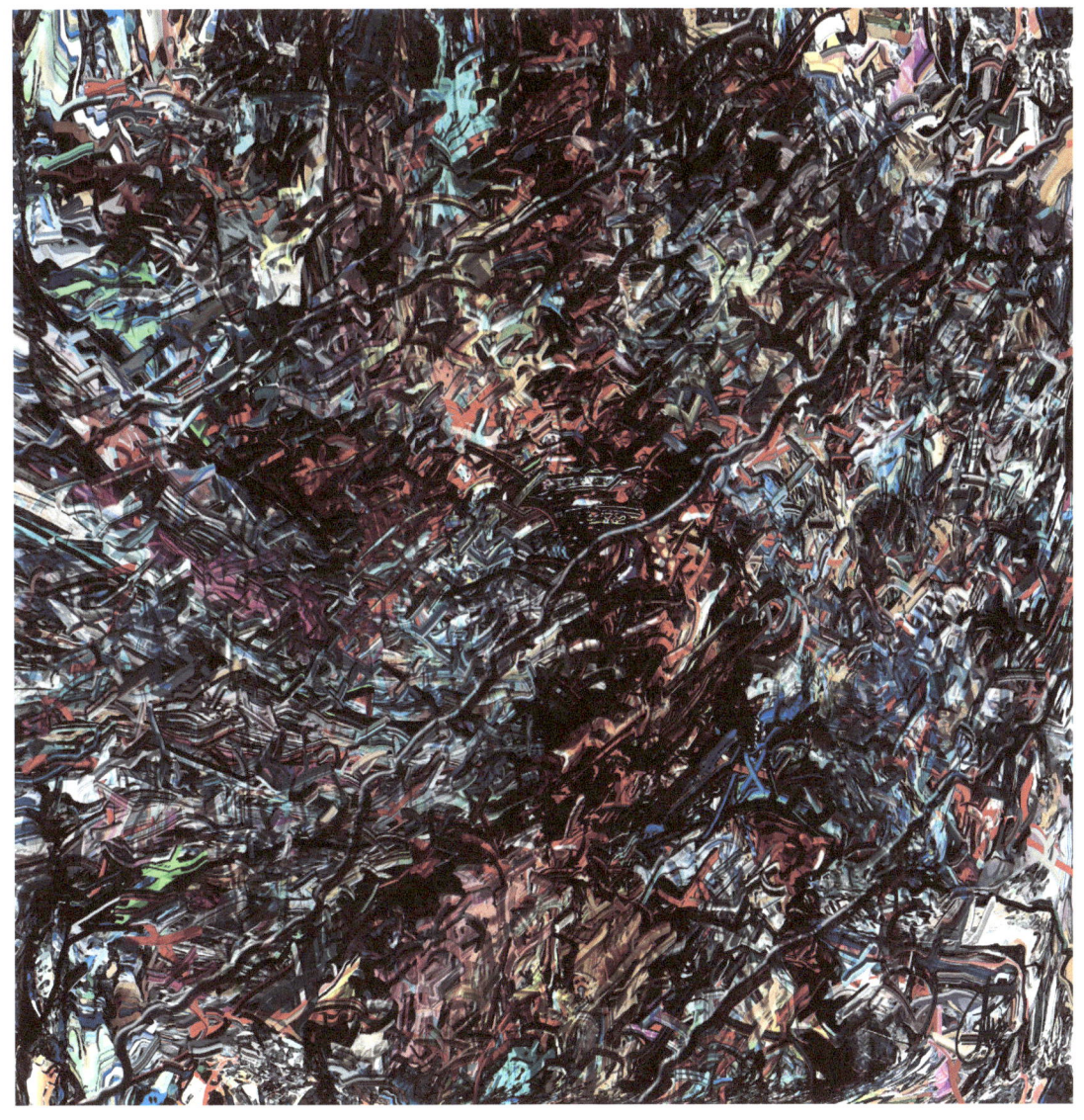

WINEWOOD

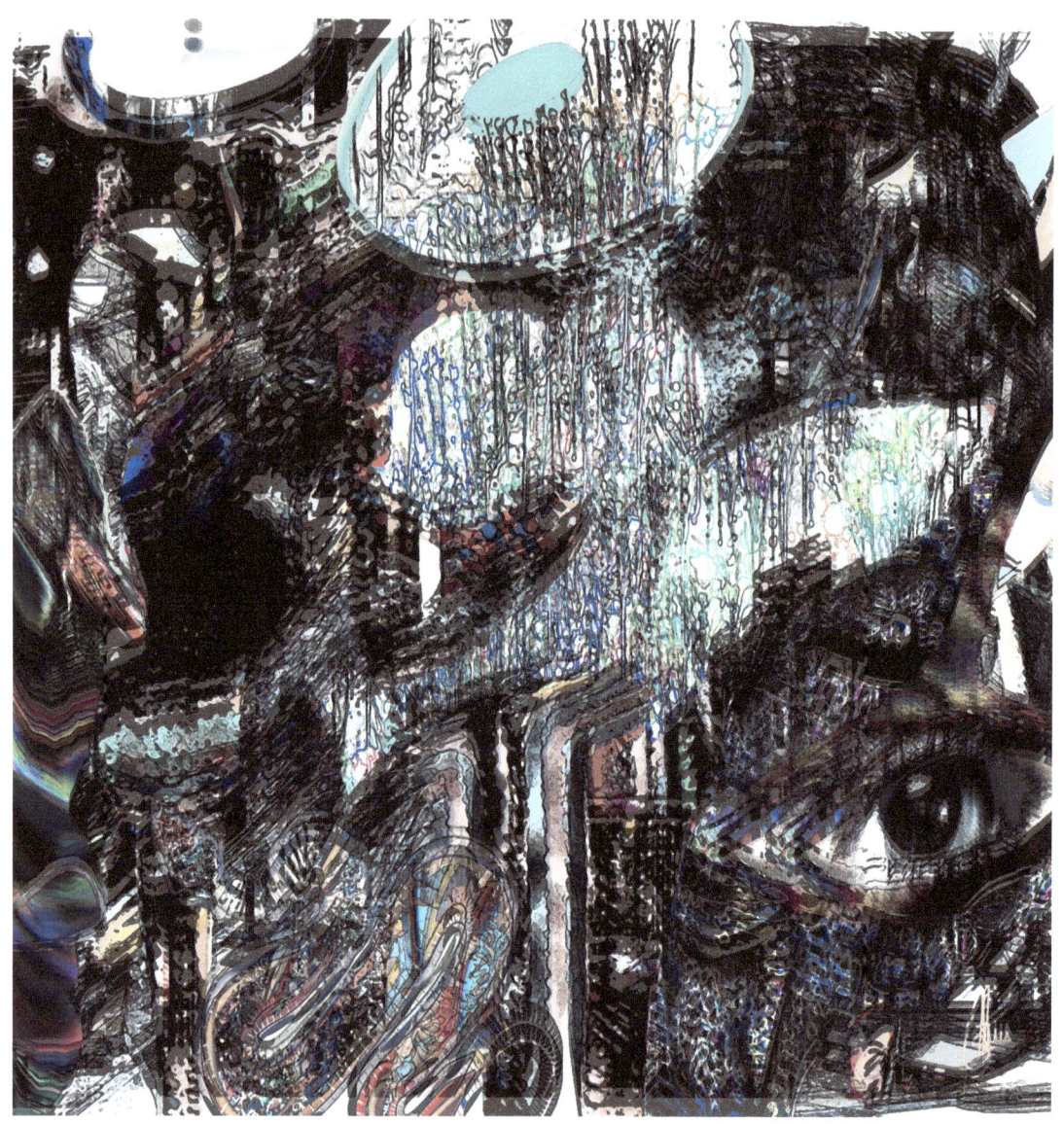

WOMAN HOLDING FISH

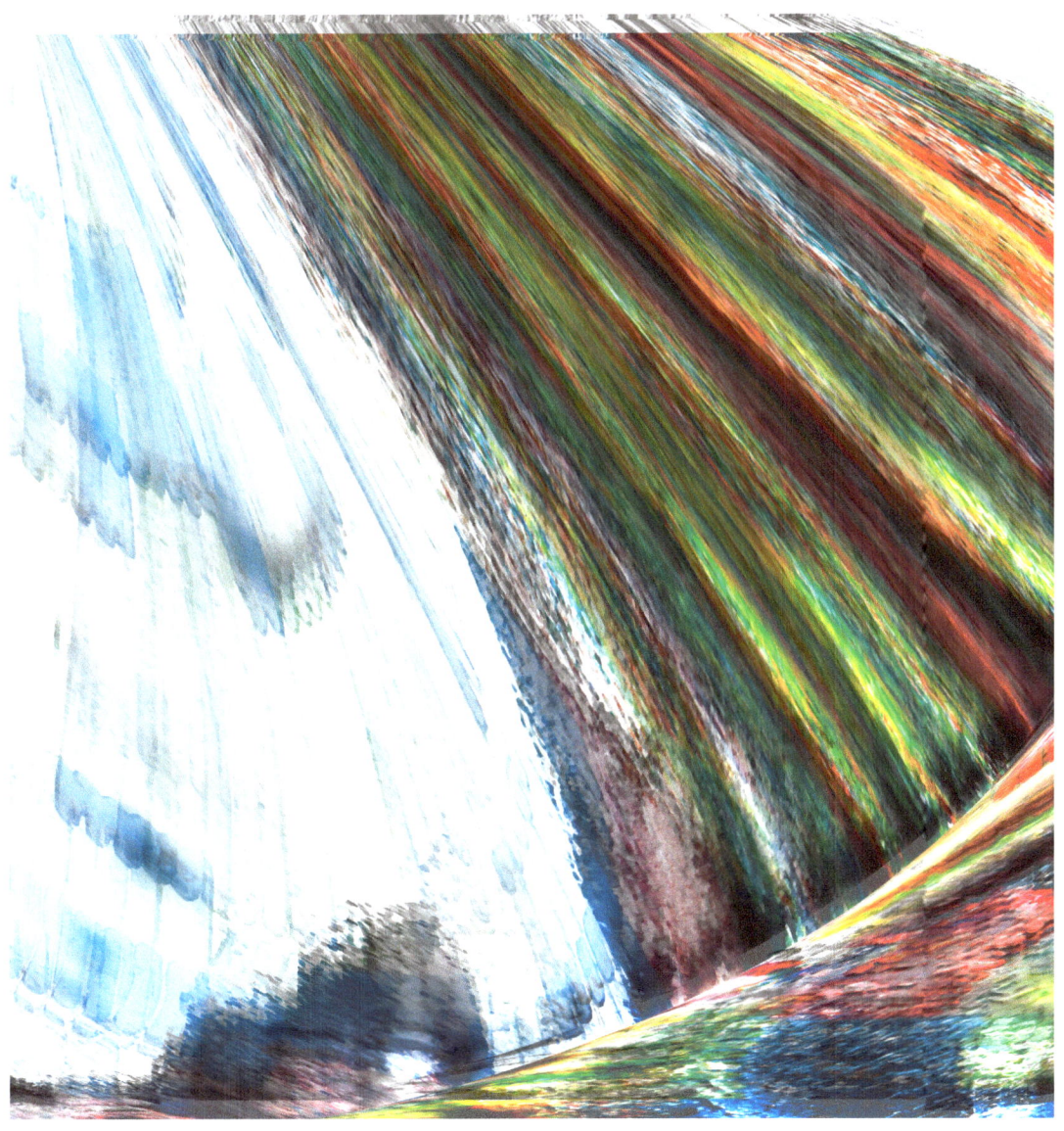

SPLASHER

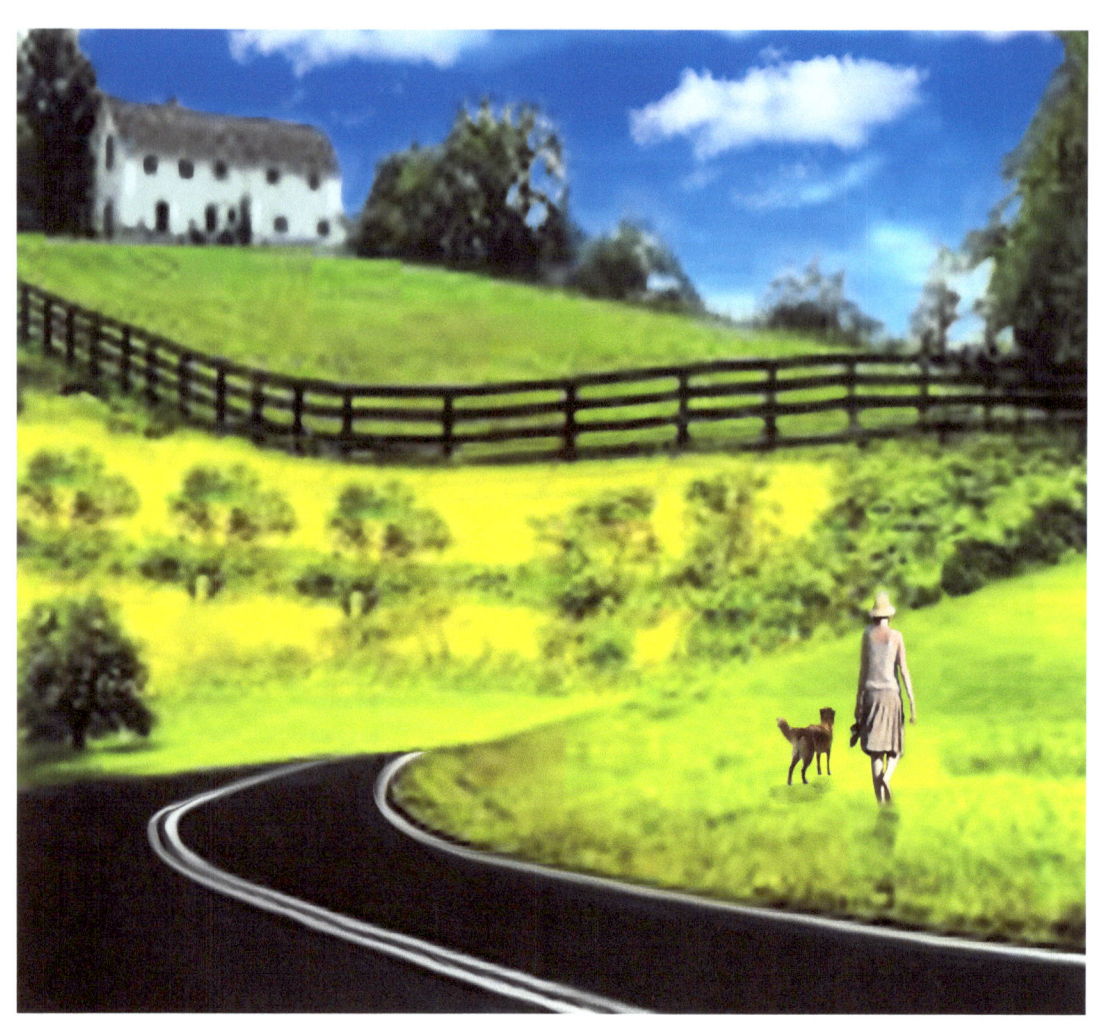

WALKING
HOME

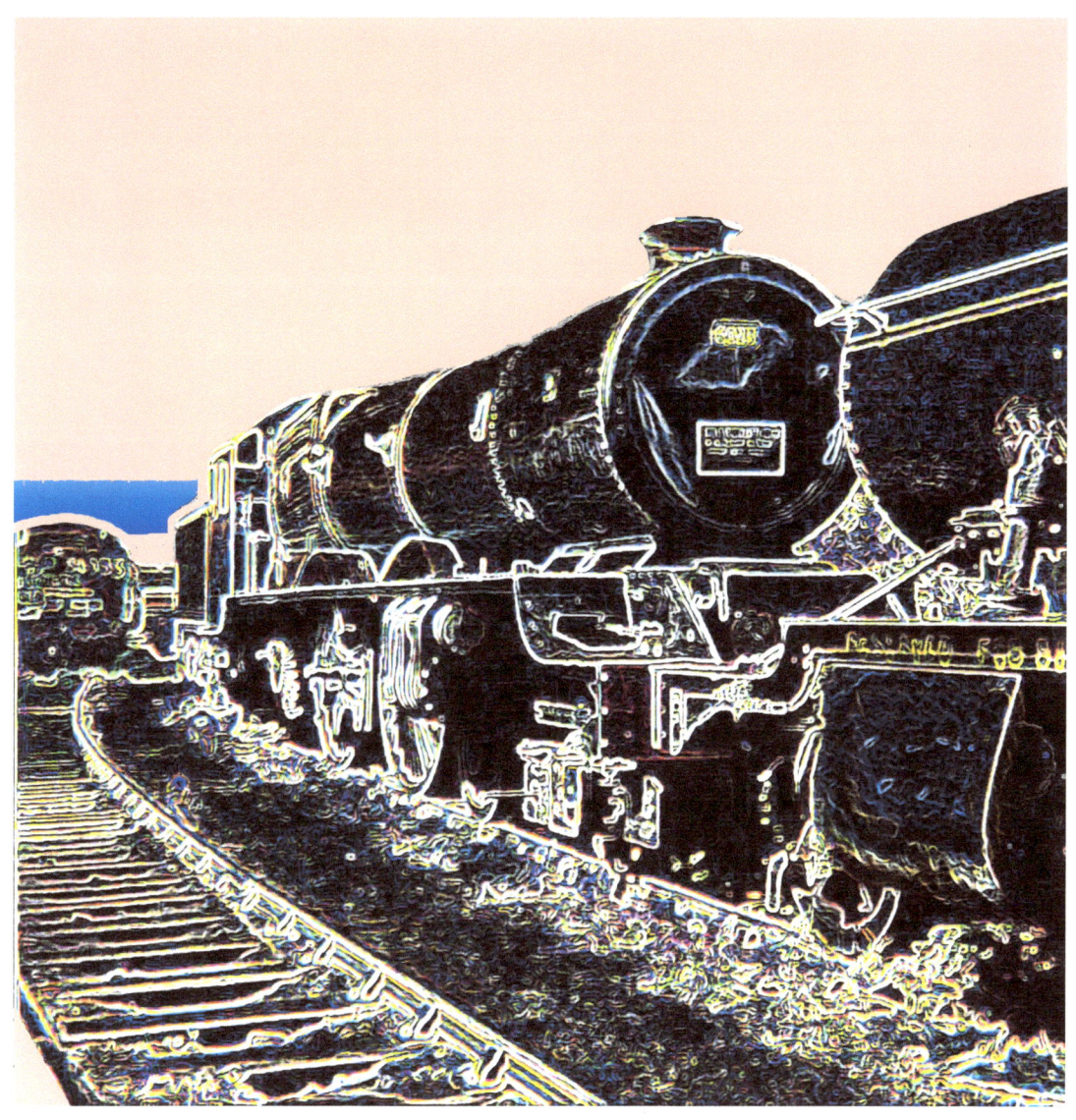

ABABDIBED
TRAIN

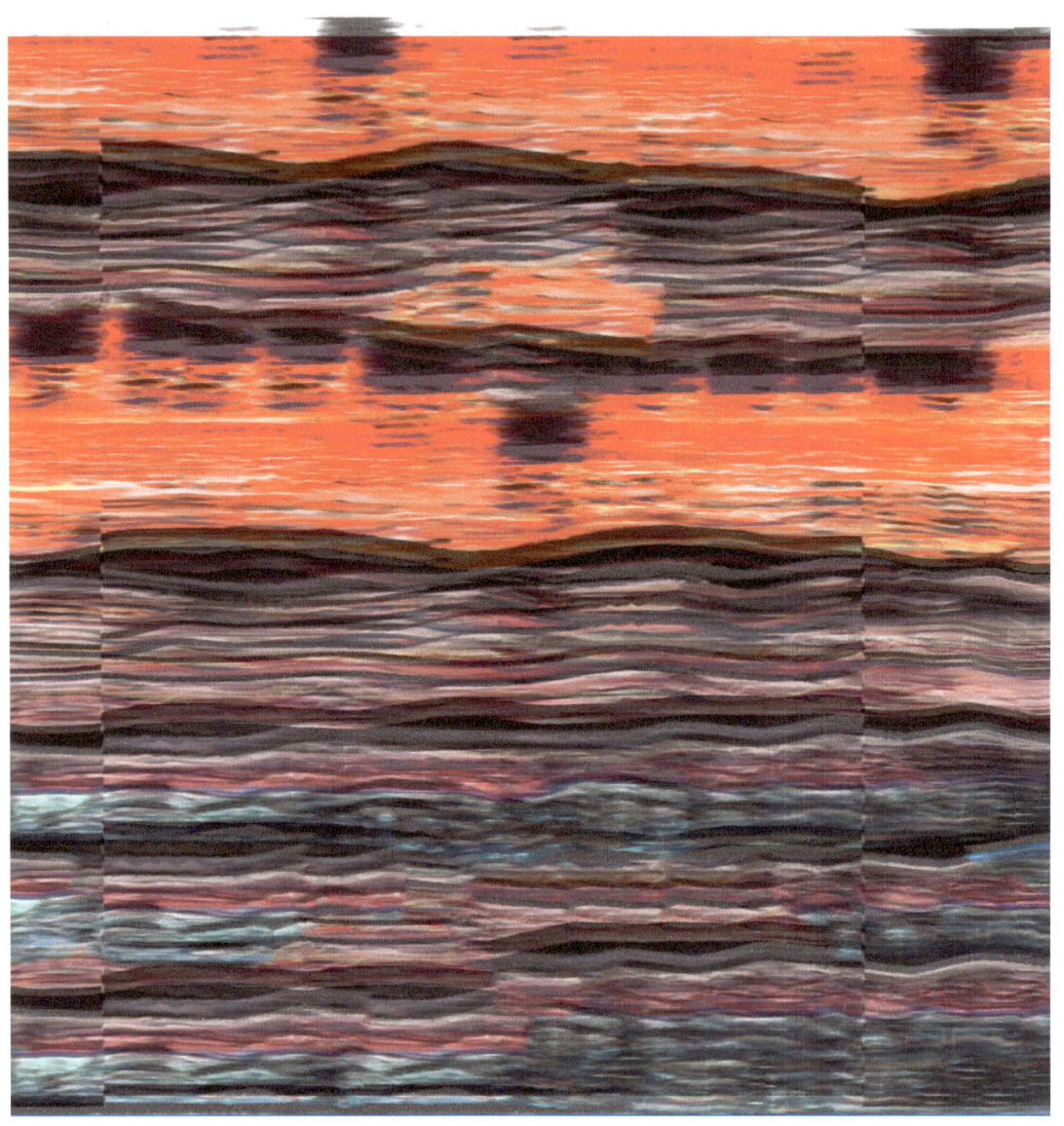

ABSTRACTEAU

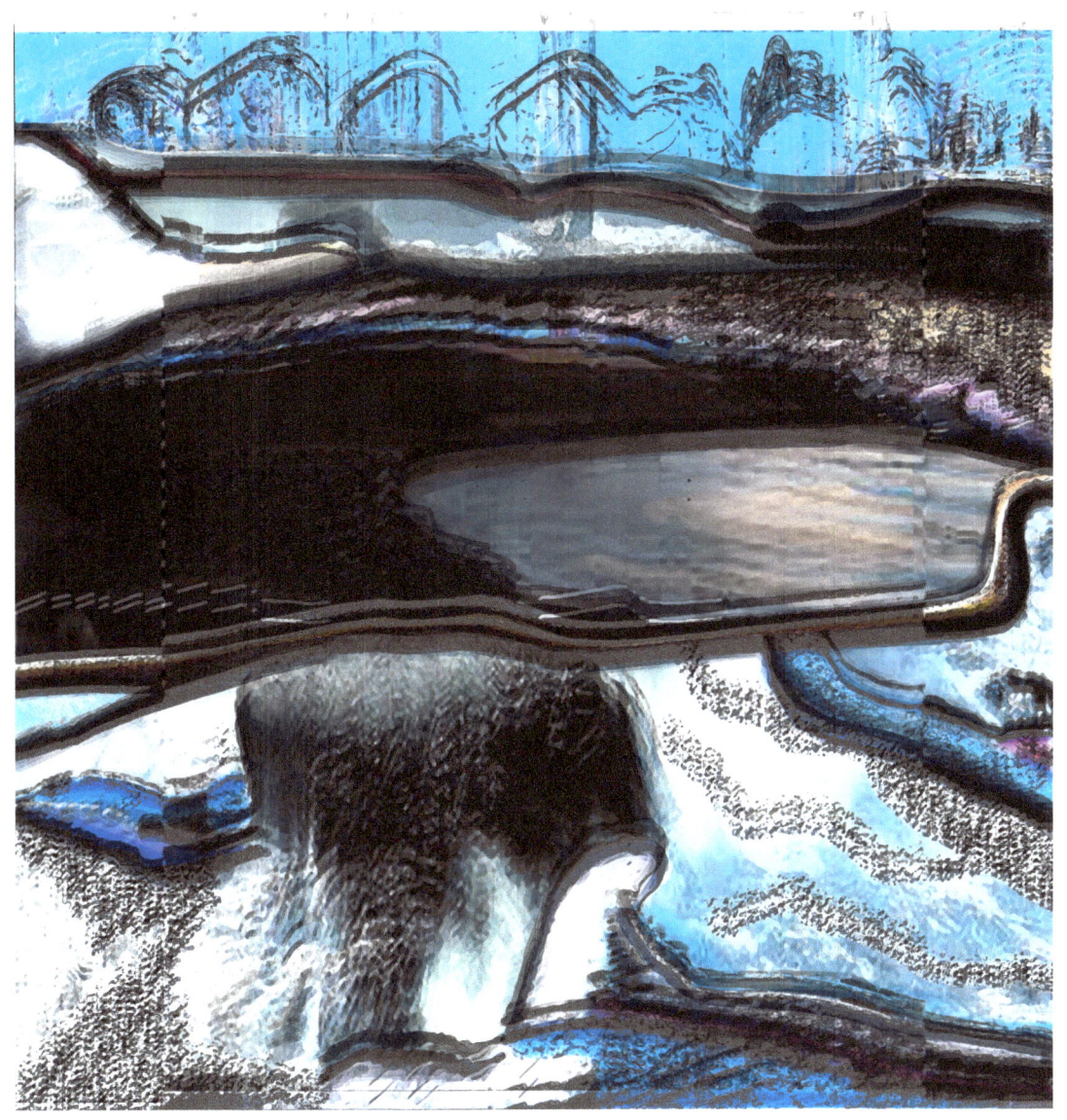

ALL TIDES
IN

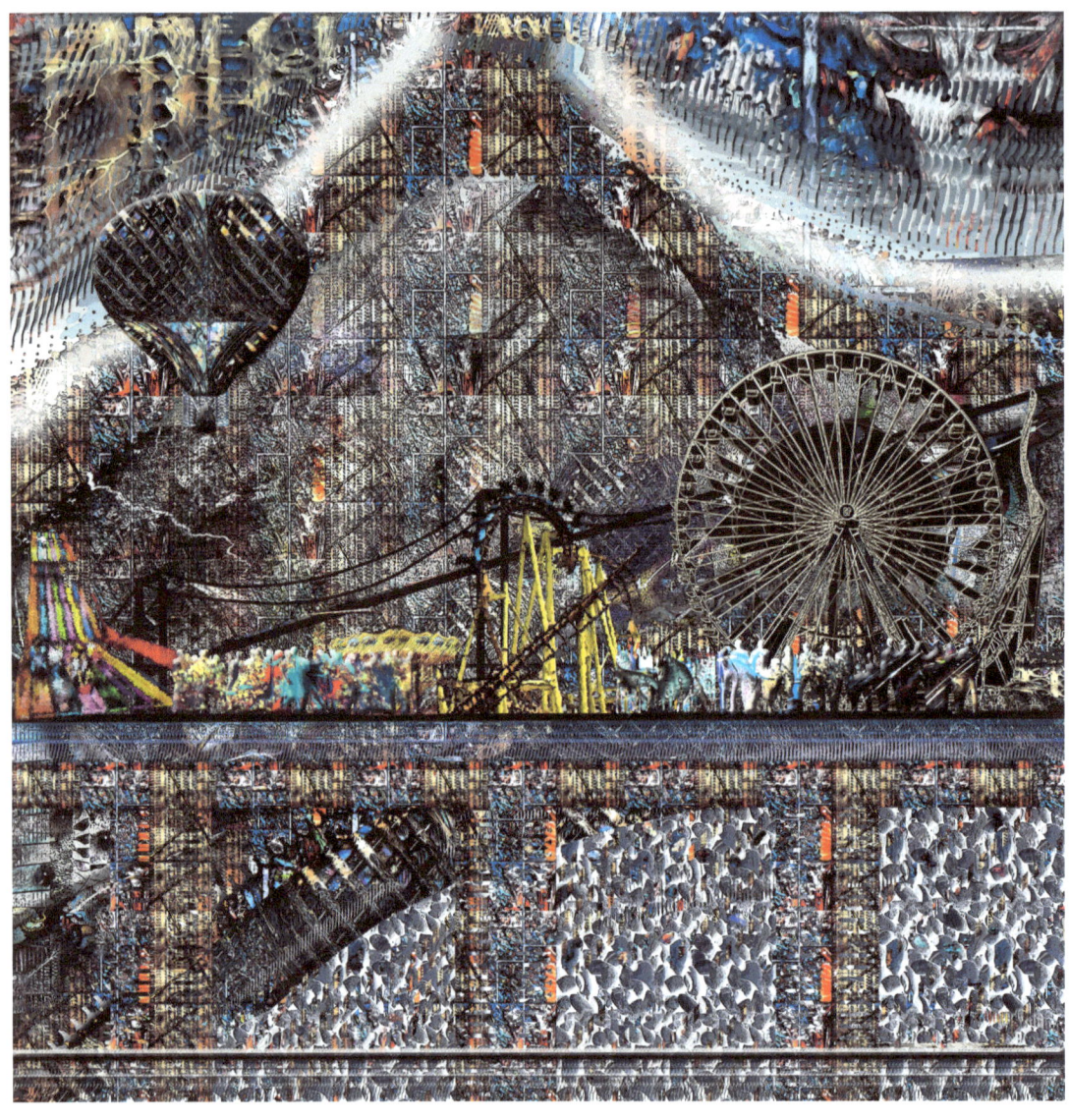

AMUSEMENT
PARK

ANATRUNK

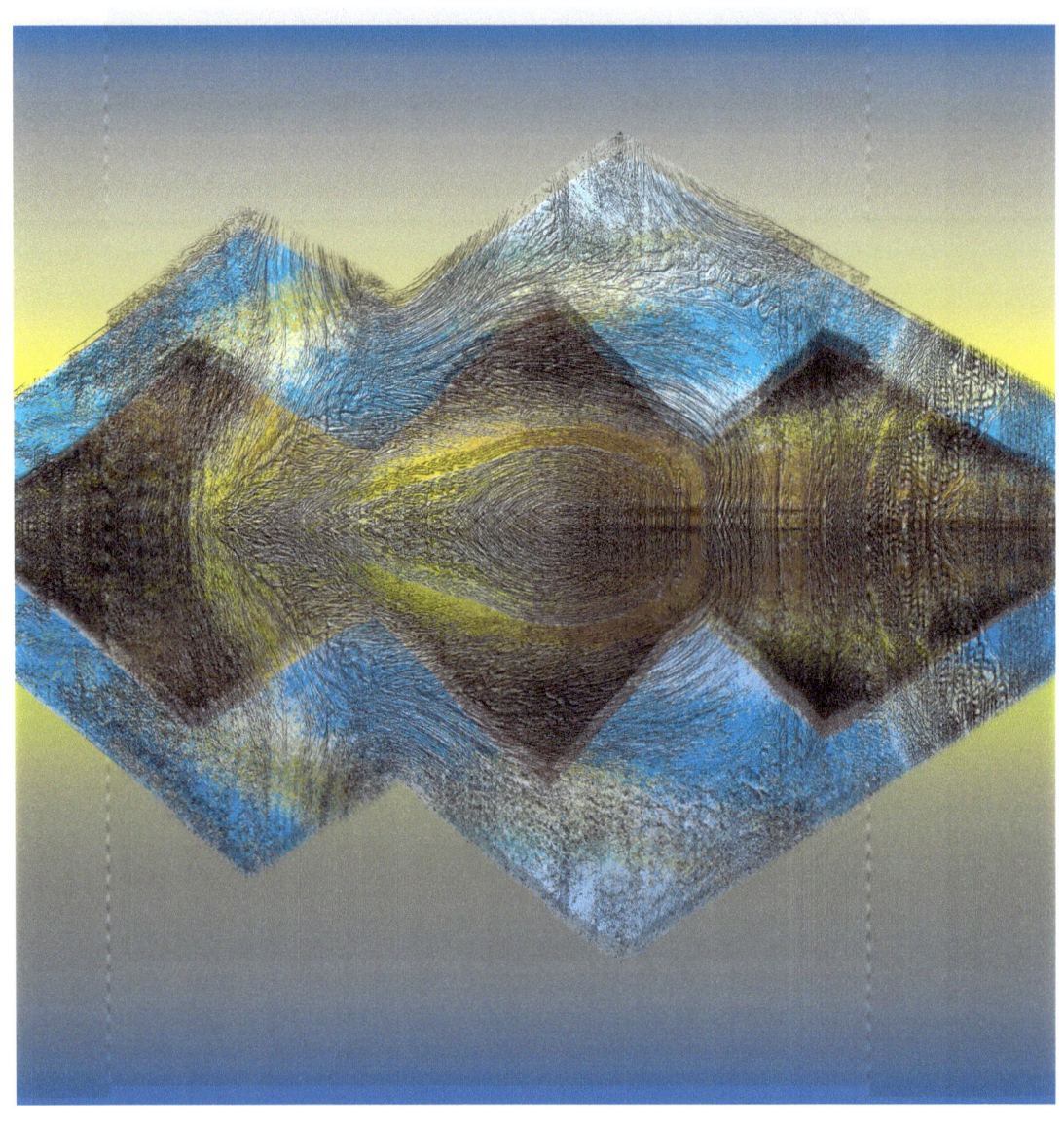

AQUAFIRMA
AQUAFIRMA

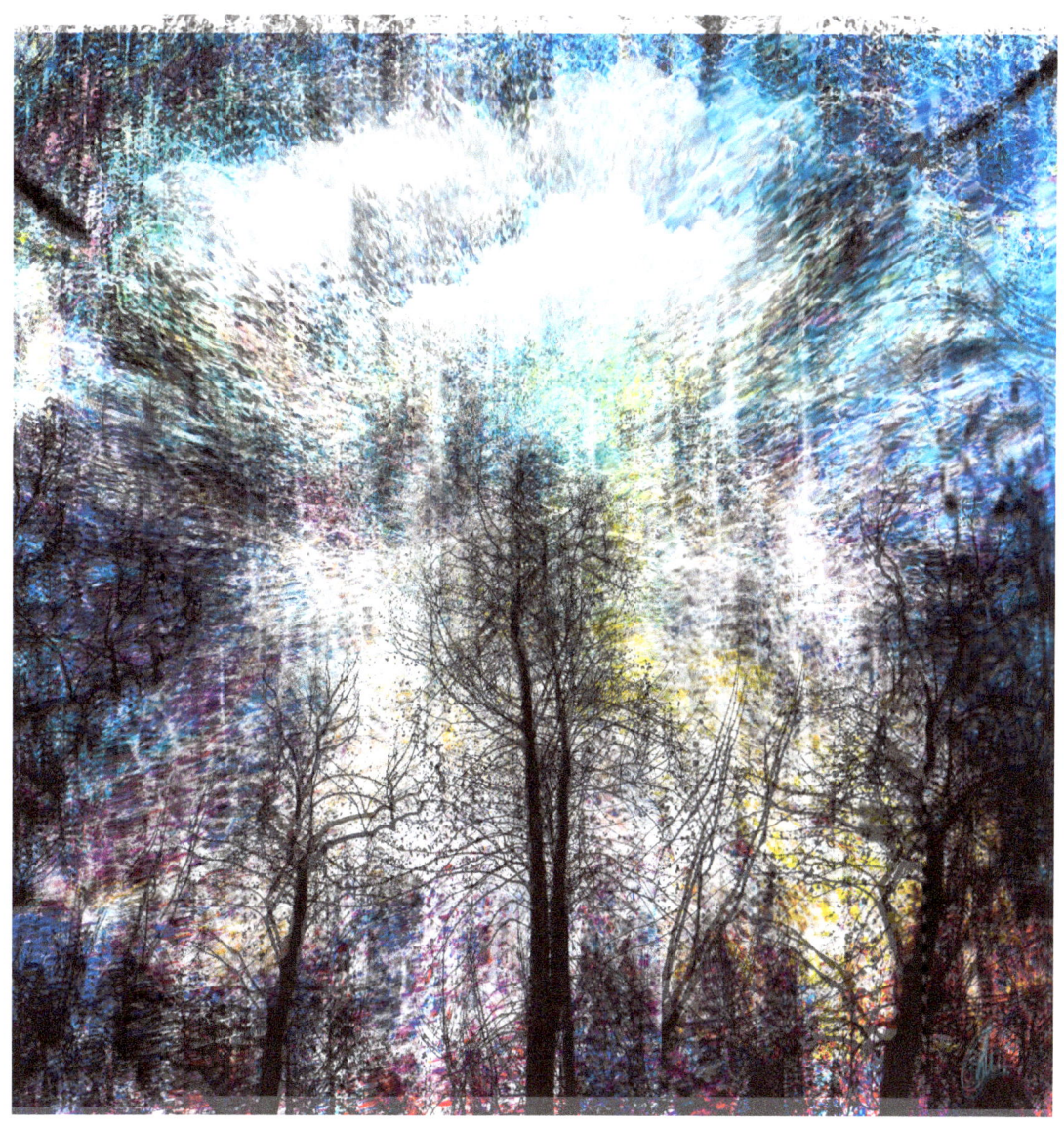

ARBOREALIS

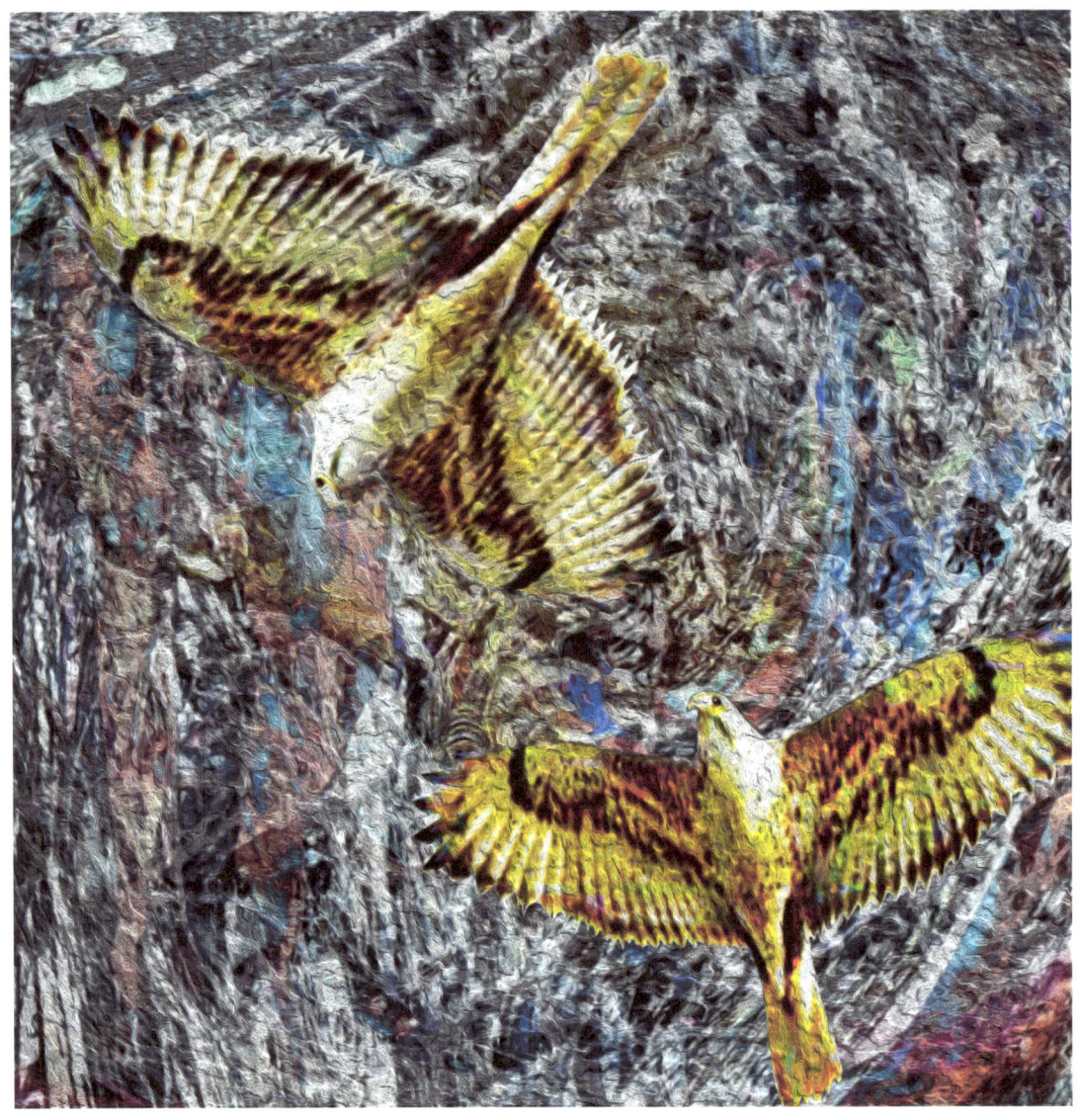

AUTERO

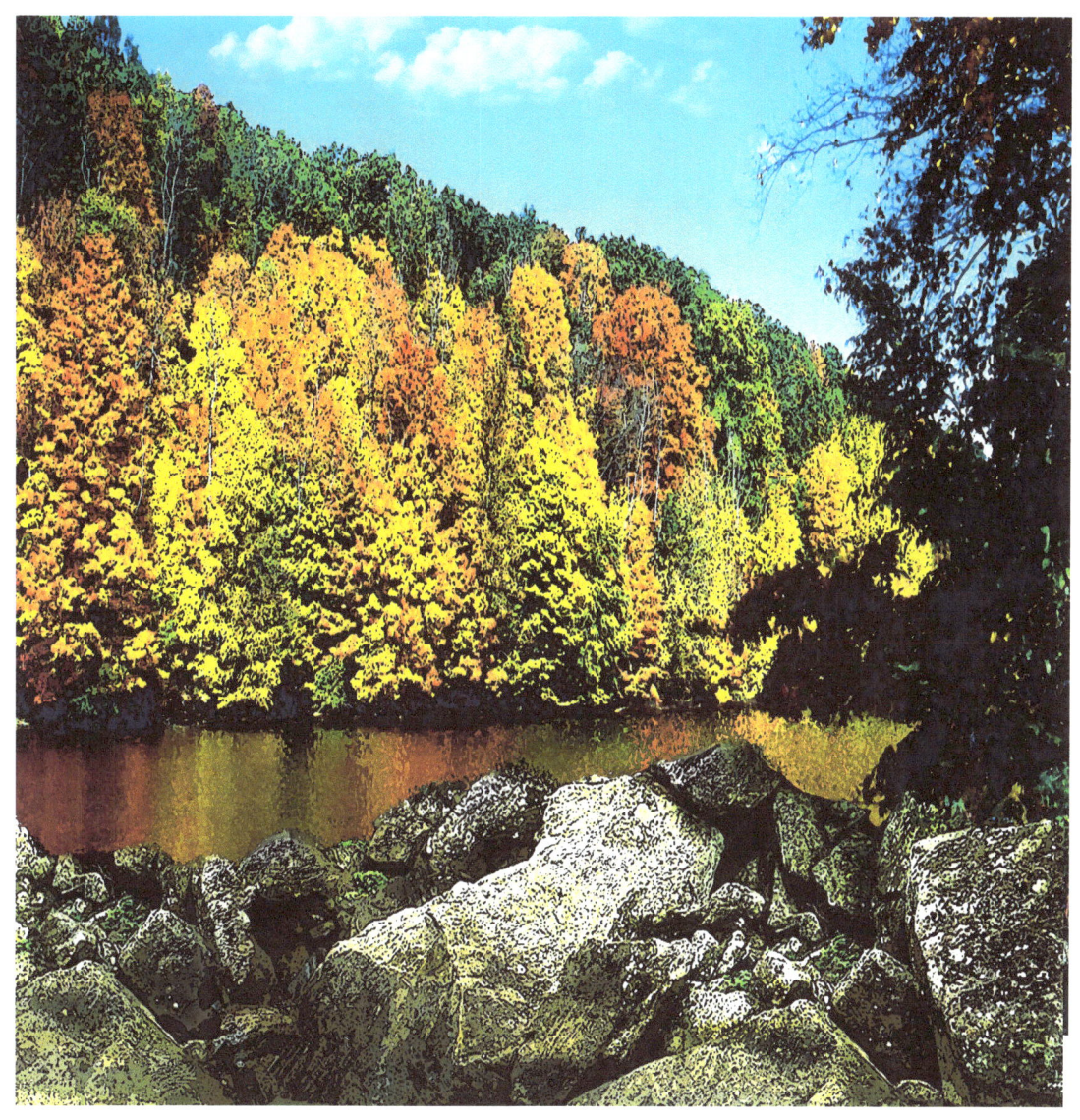

AUTUMN
LAKE

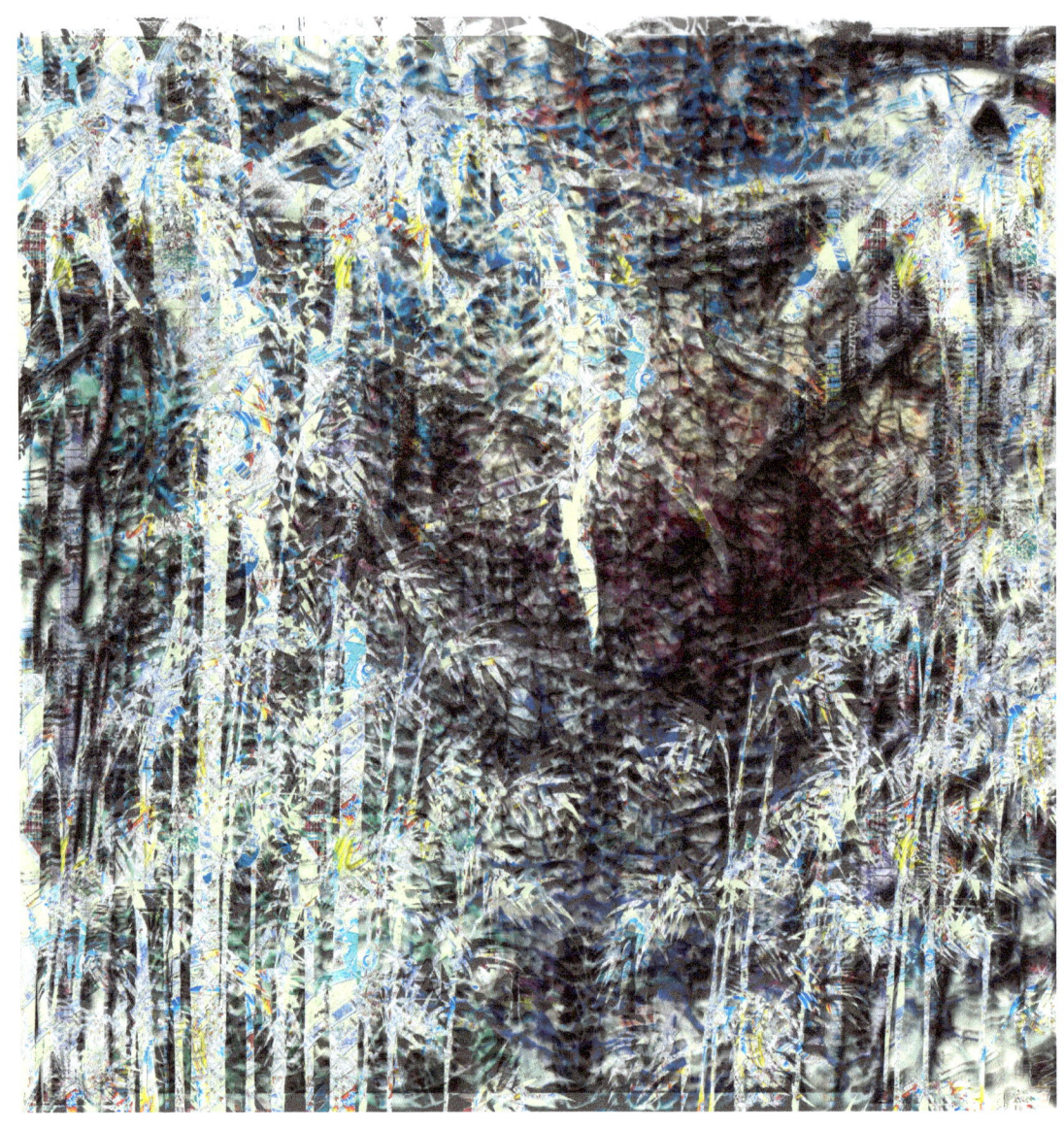

BAMBOOLI

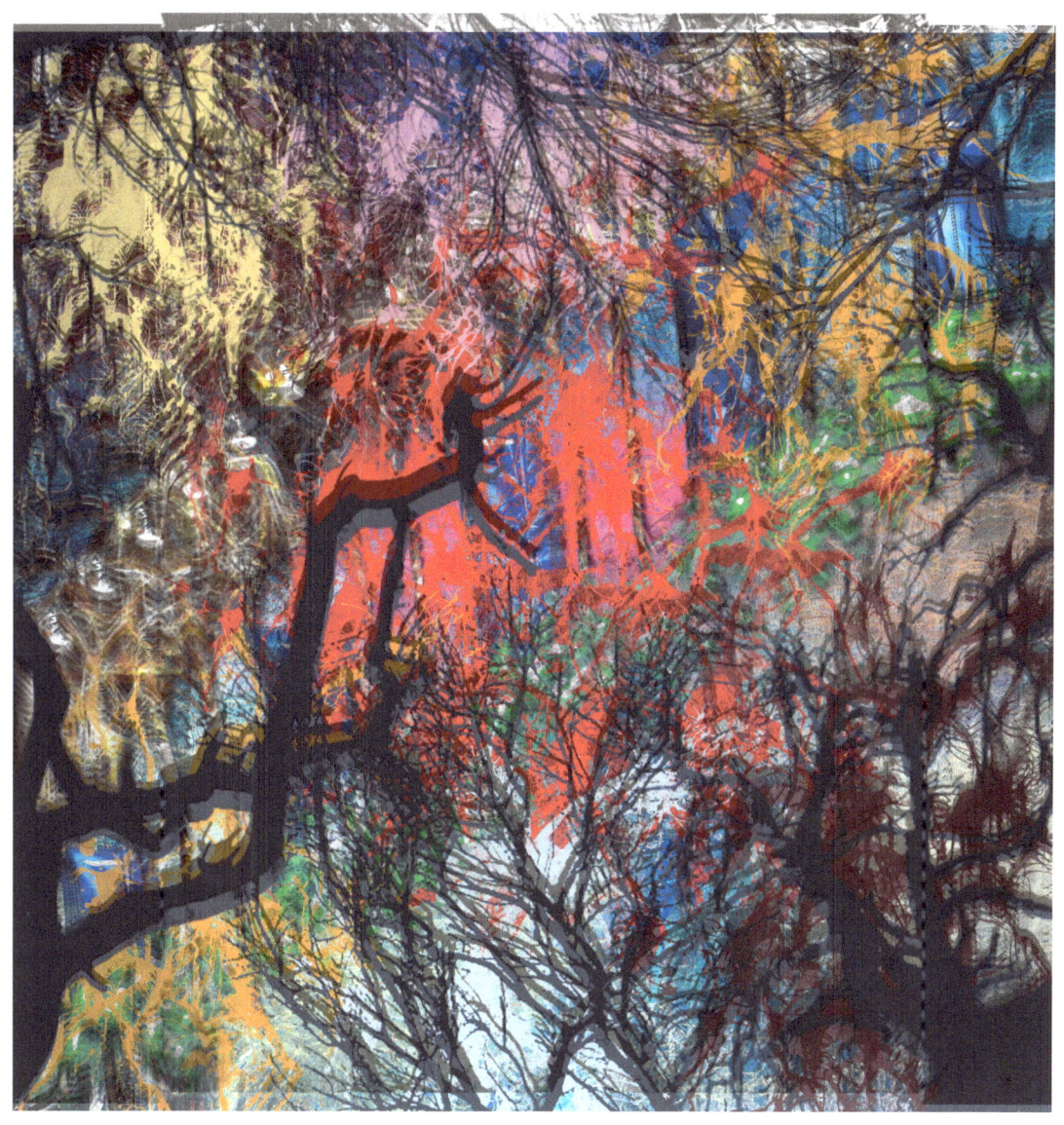

BARKIBEAU

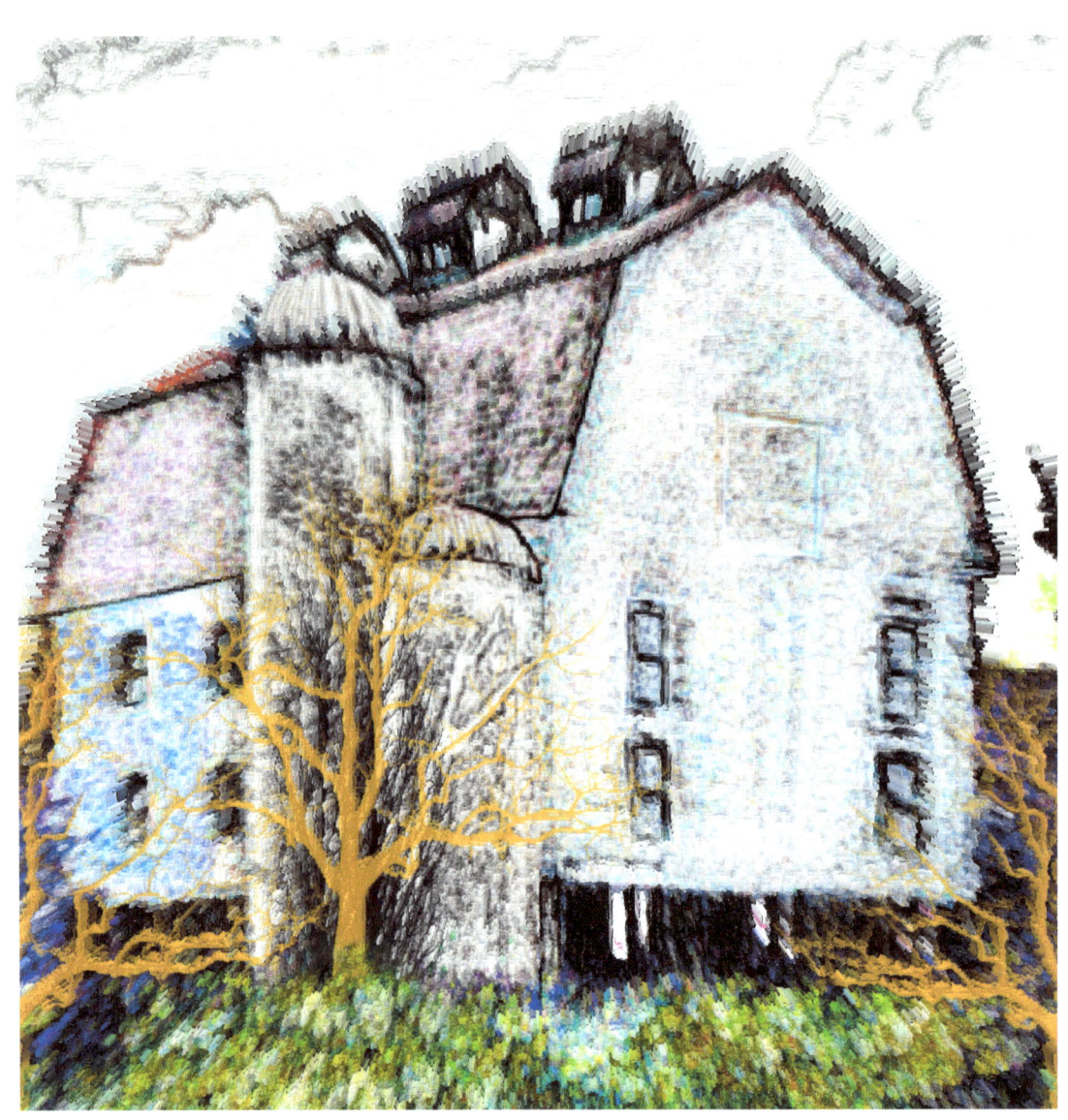

BARN WITH SILOS

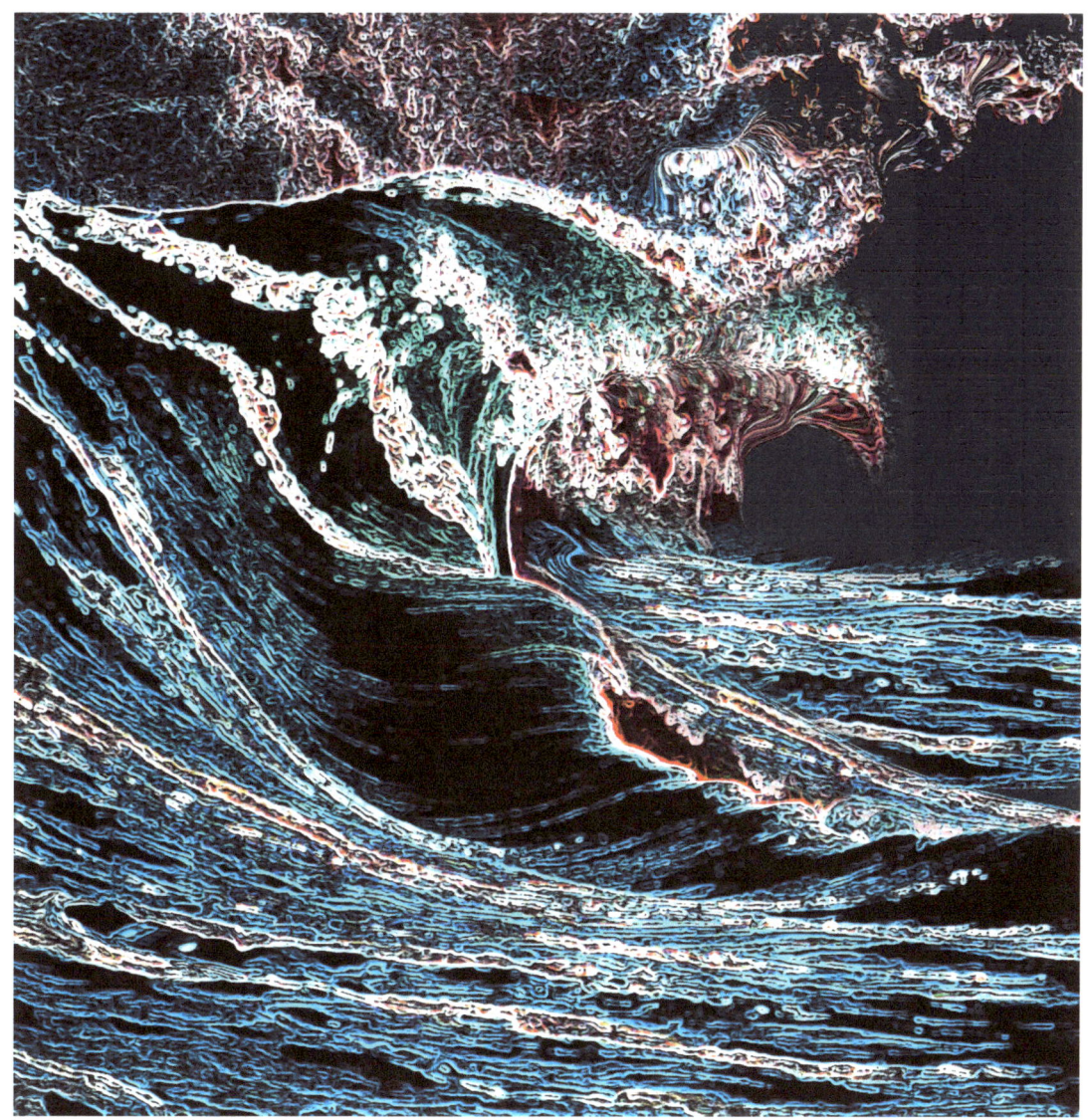

BIG
SUR

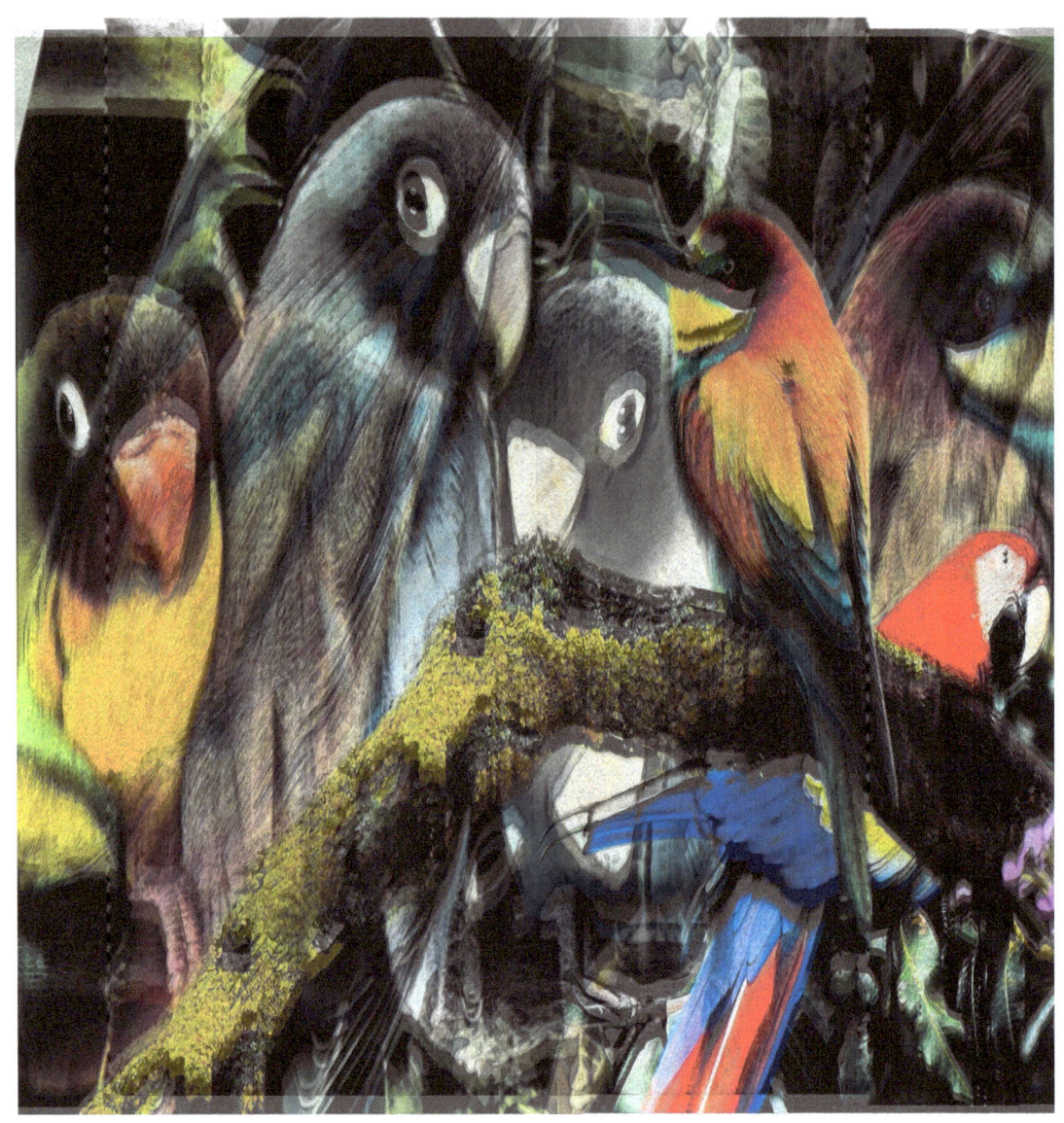

BIRD GATHERING

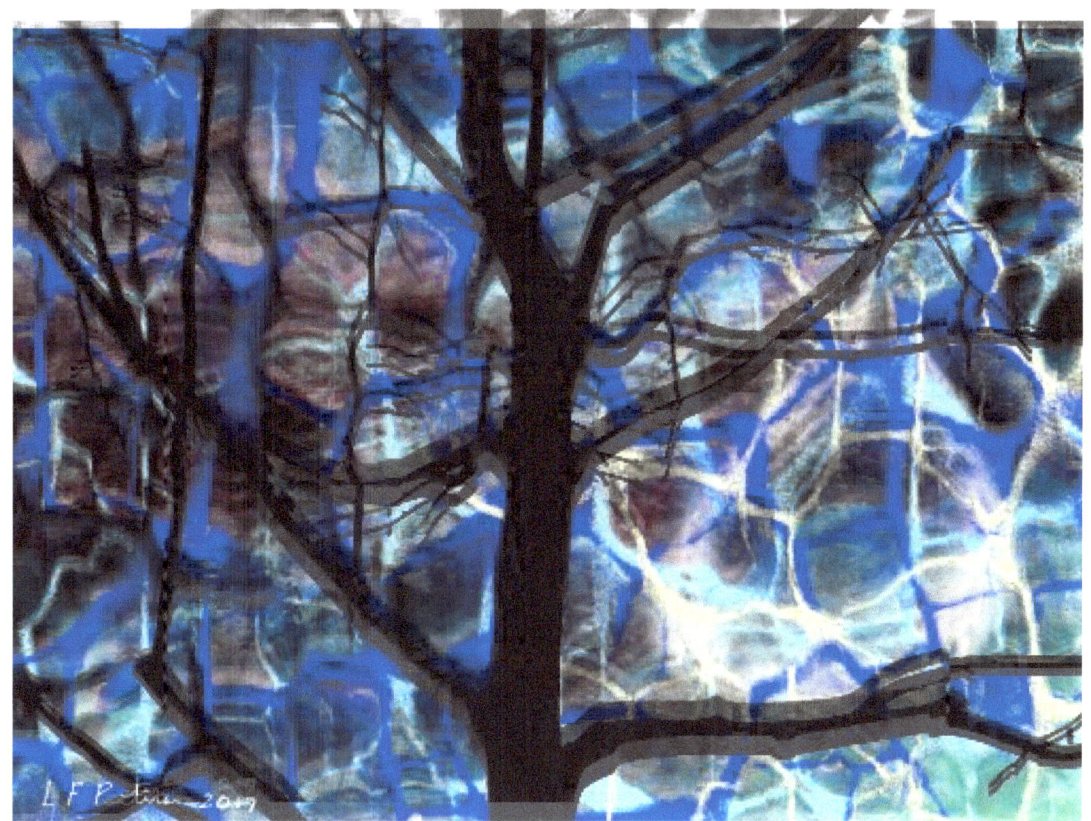

BLACK
TREE

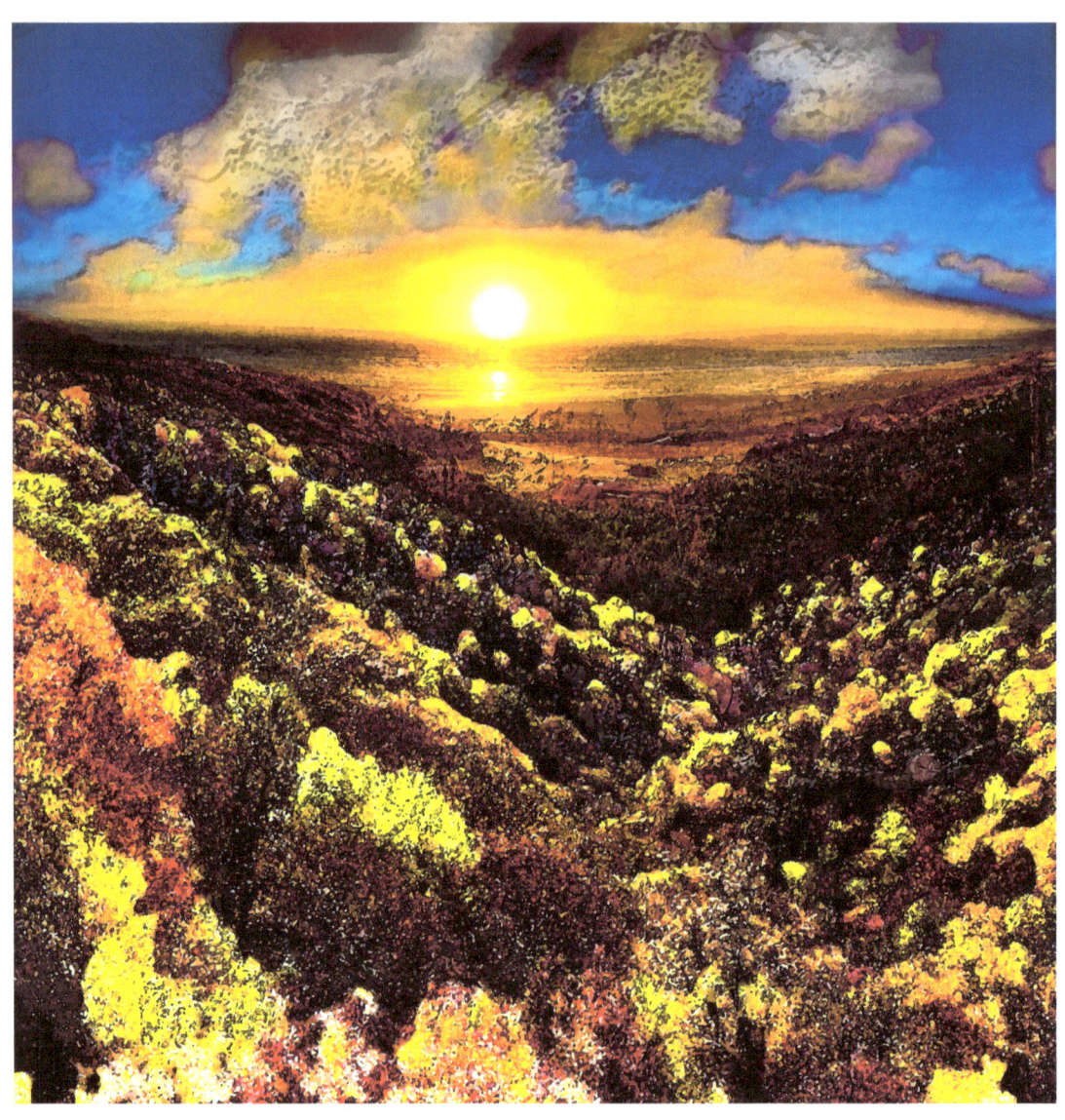

BLAZING SUNSET

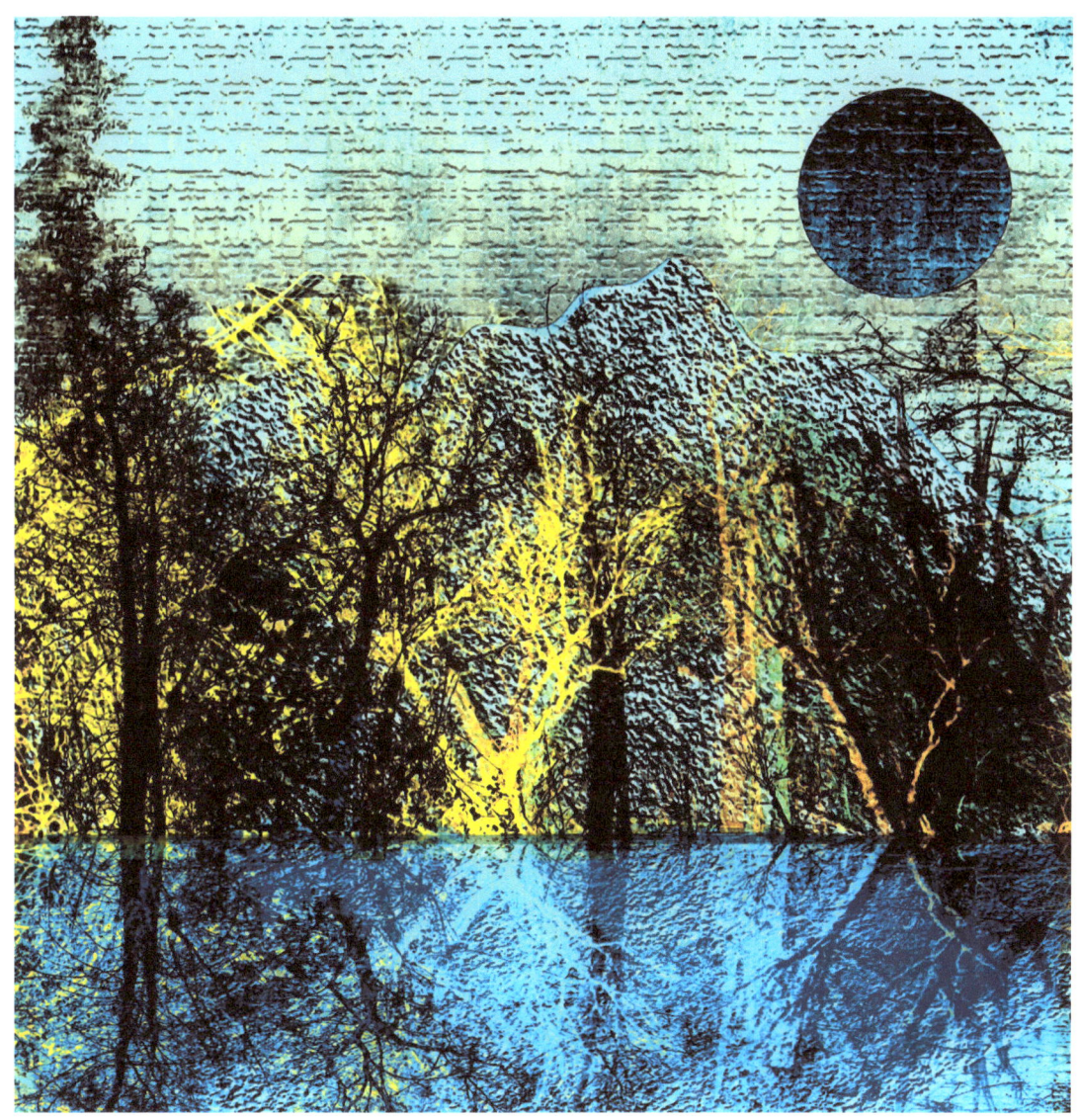

BLUE
MOON

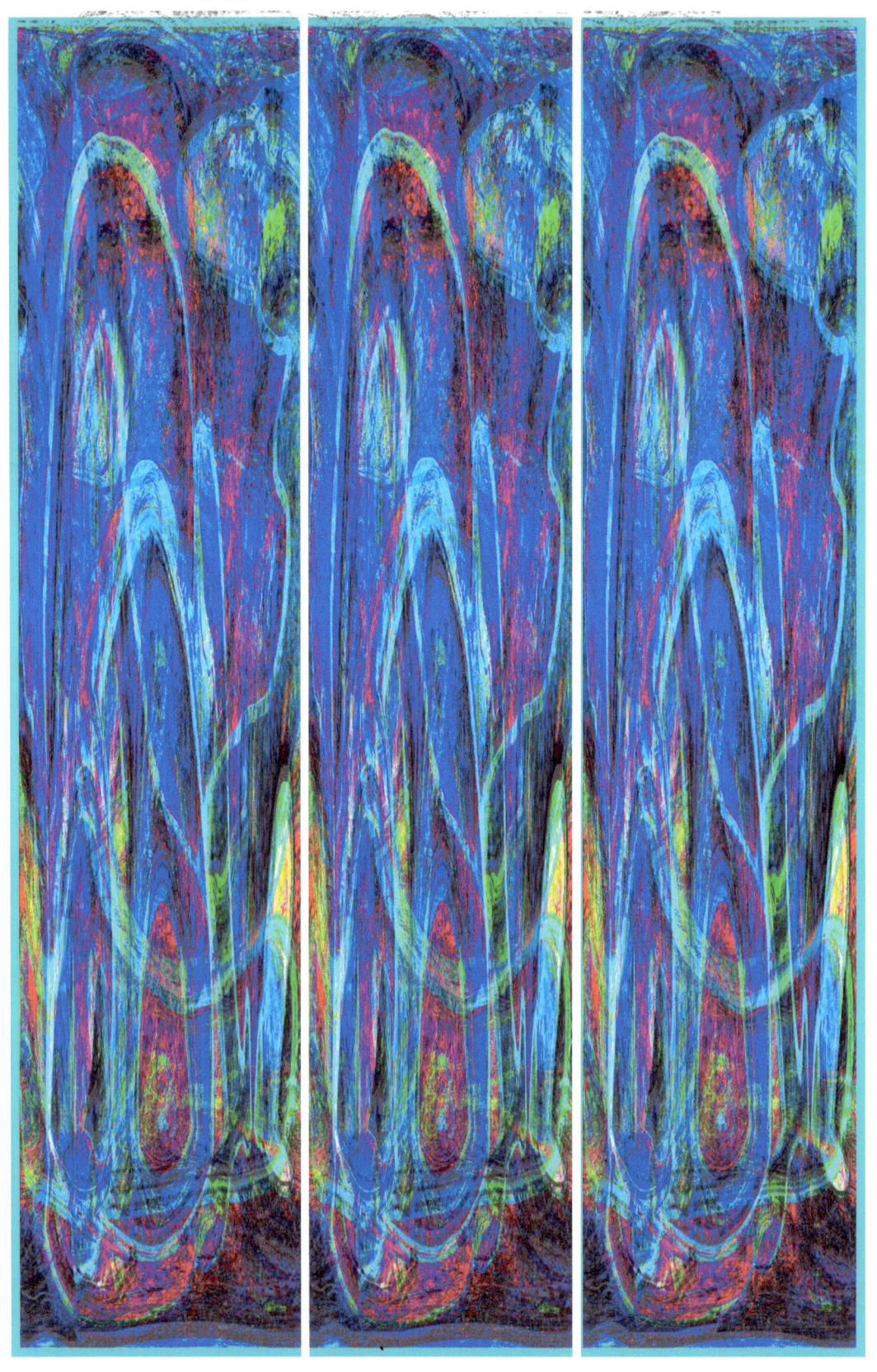

BLUE PANELS

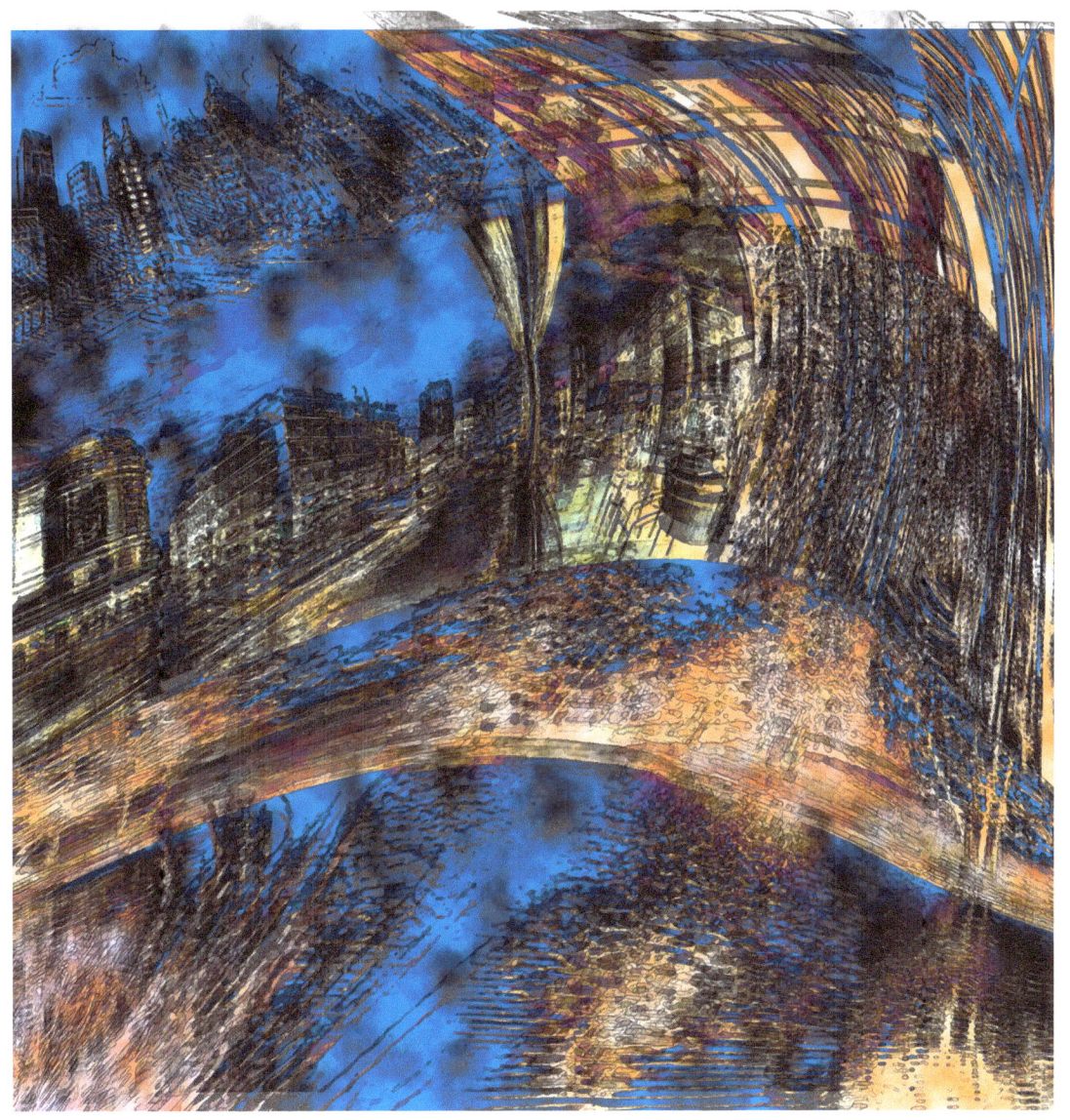

BON
CITY

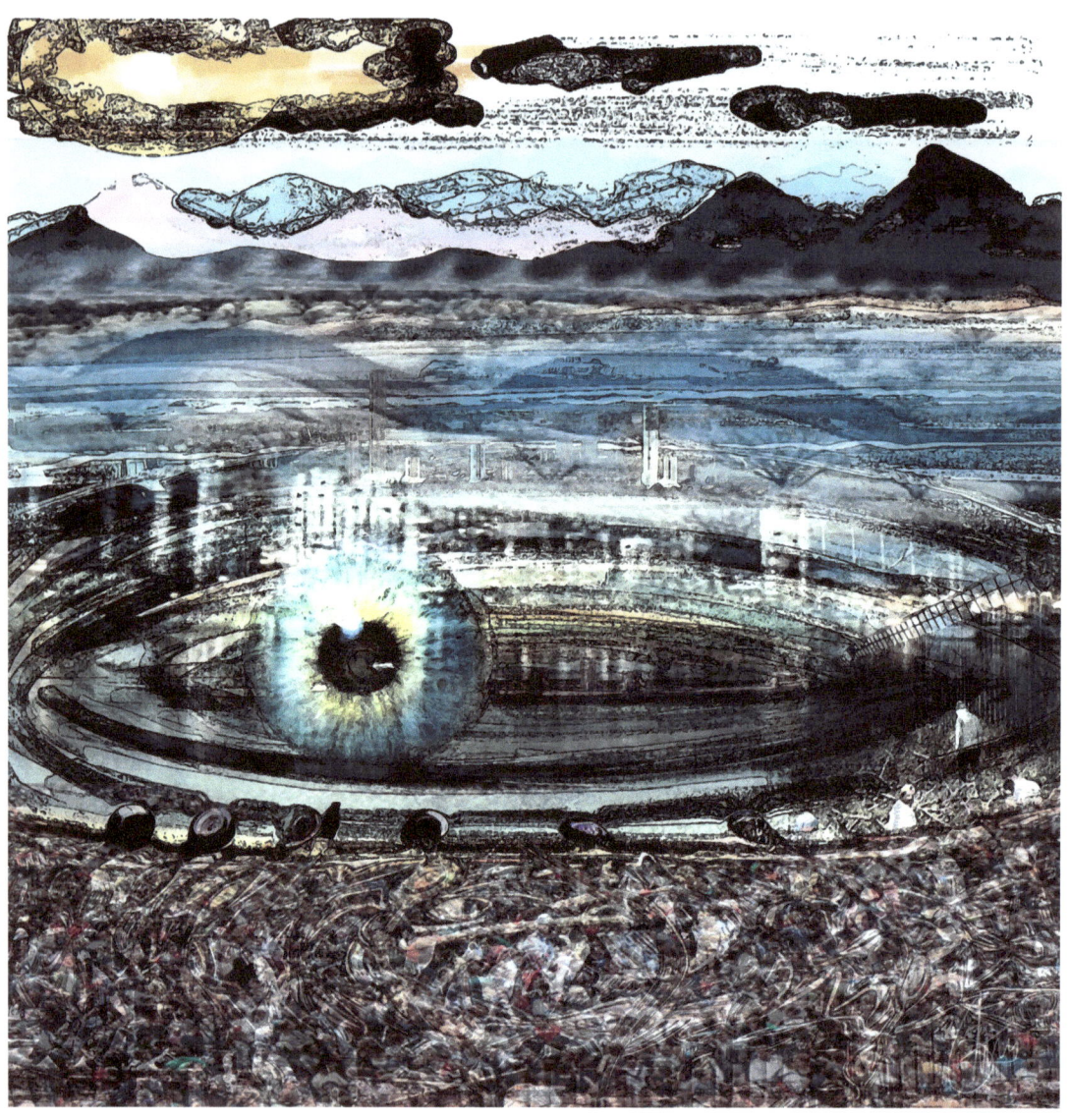

BORDER FENCE

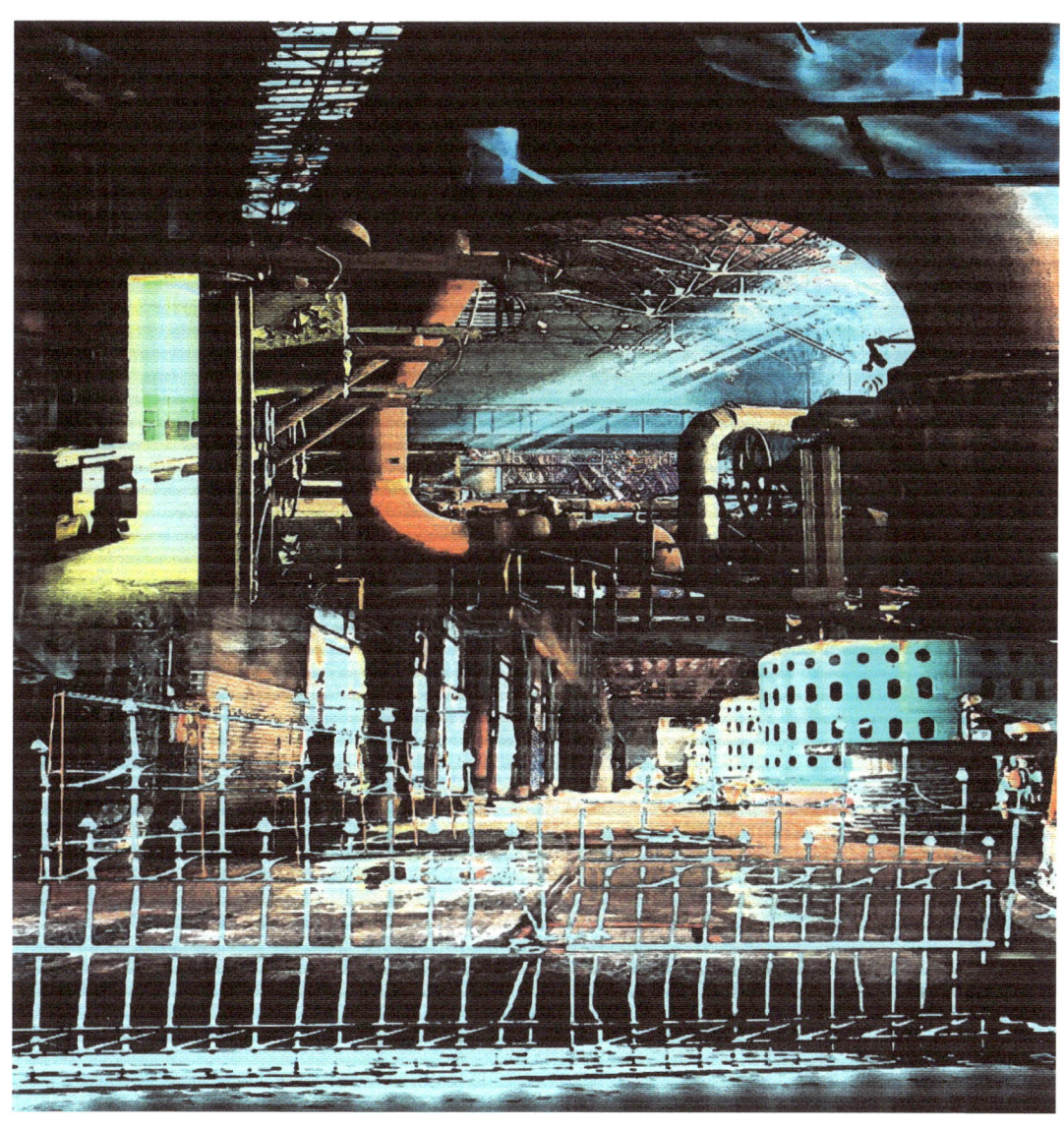

Border Gate

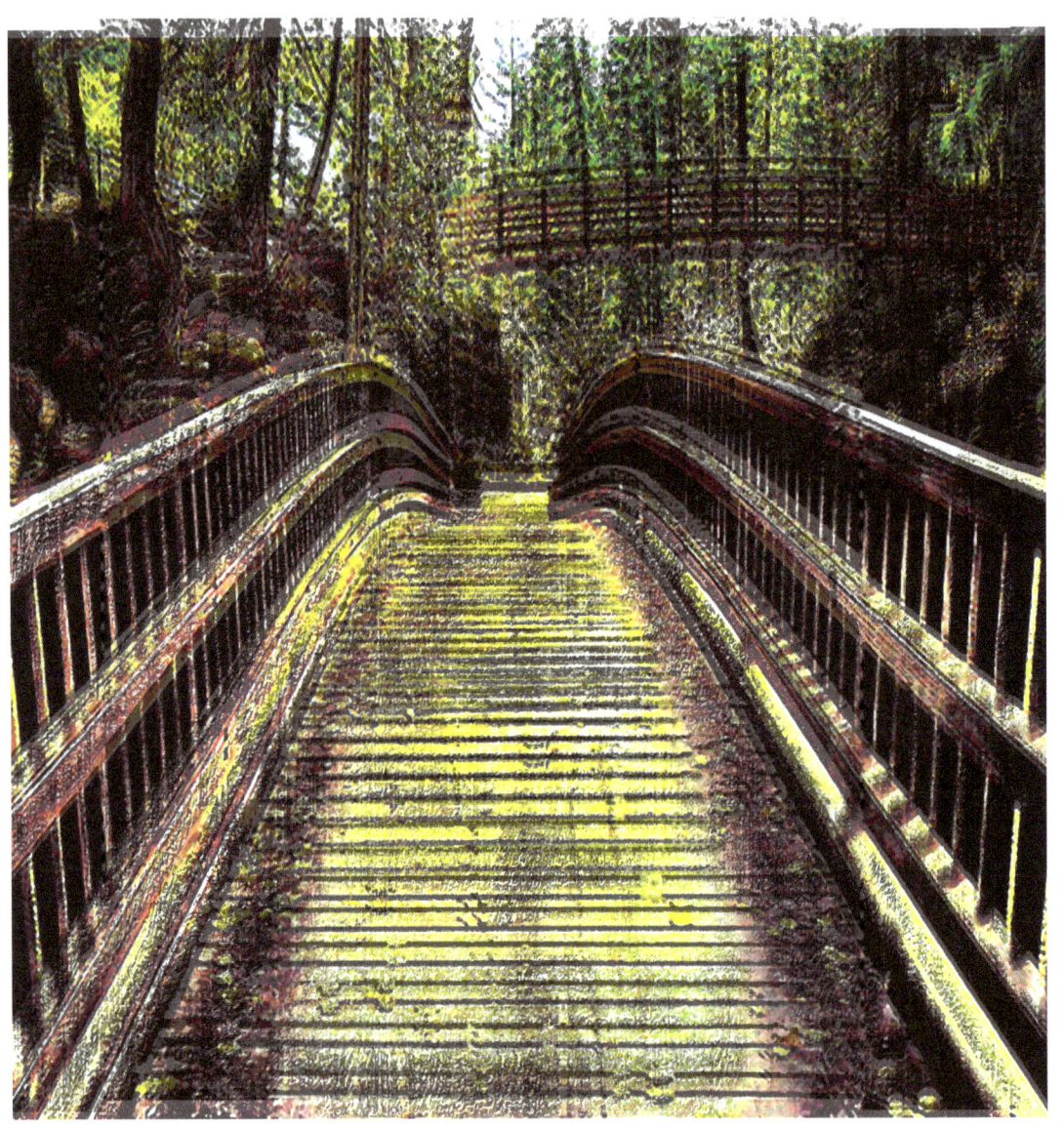

Bridge In Forest

Bridge Over Creek

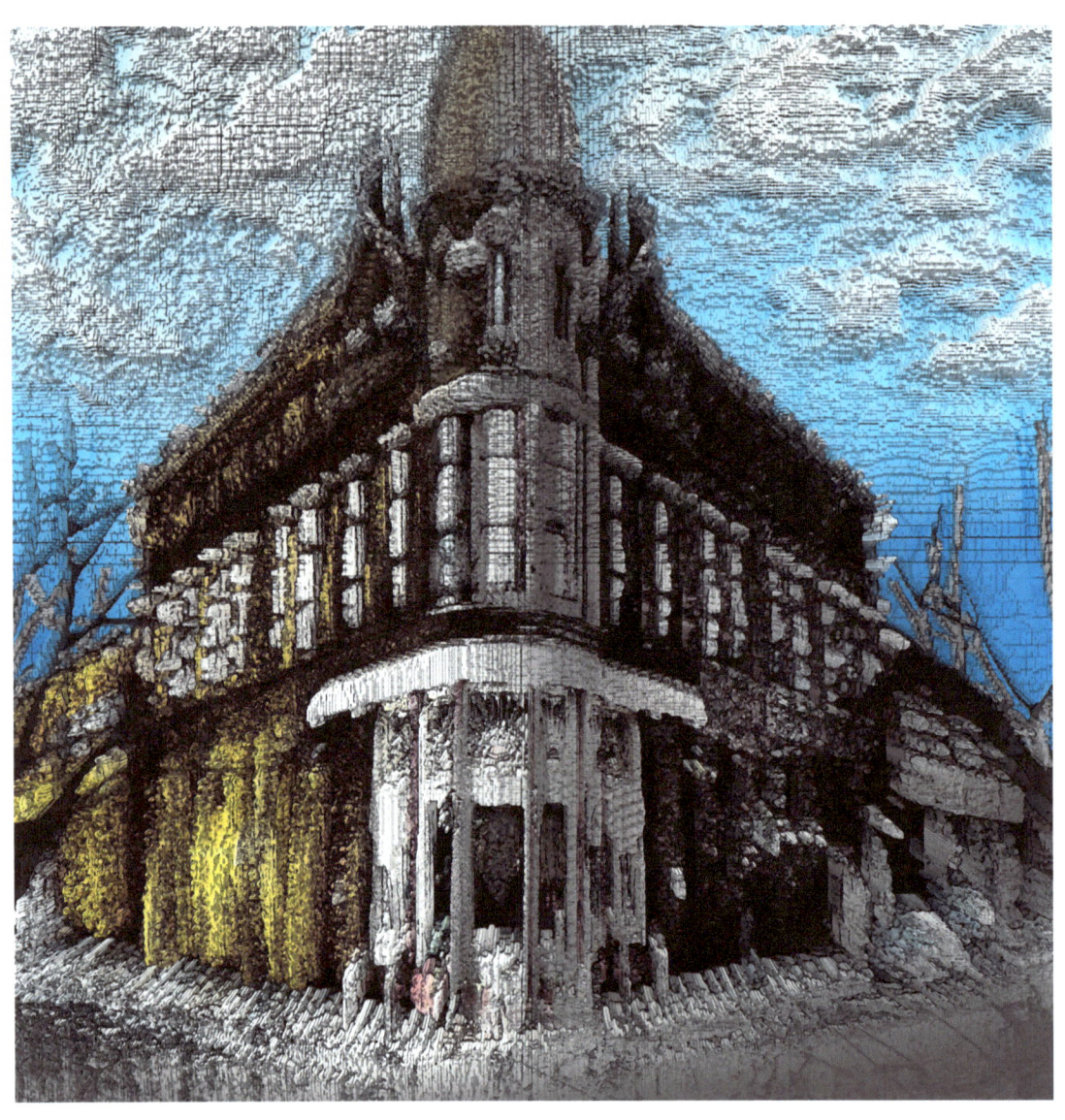

Building Wedge

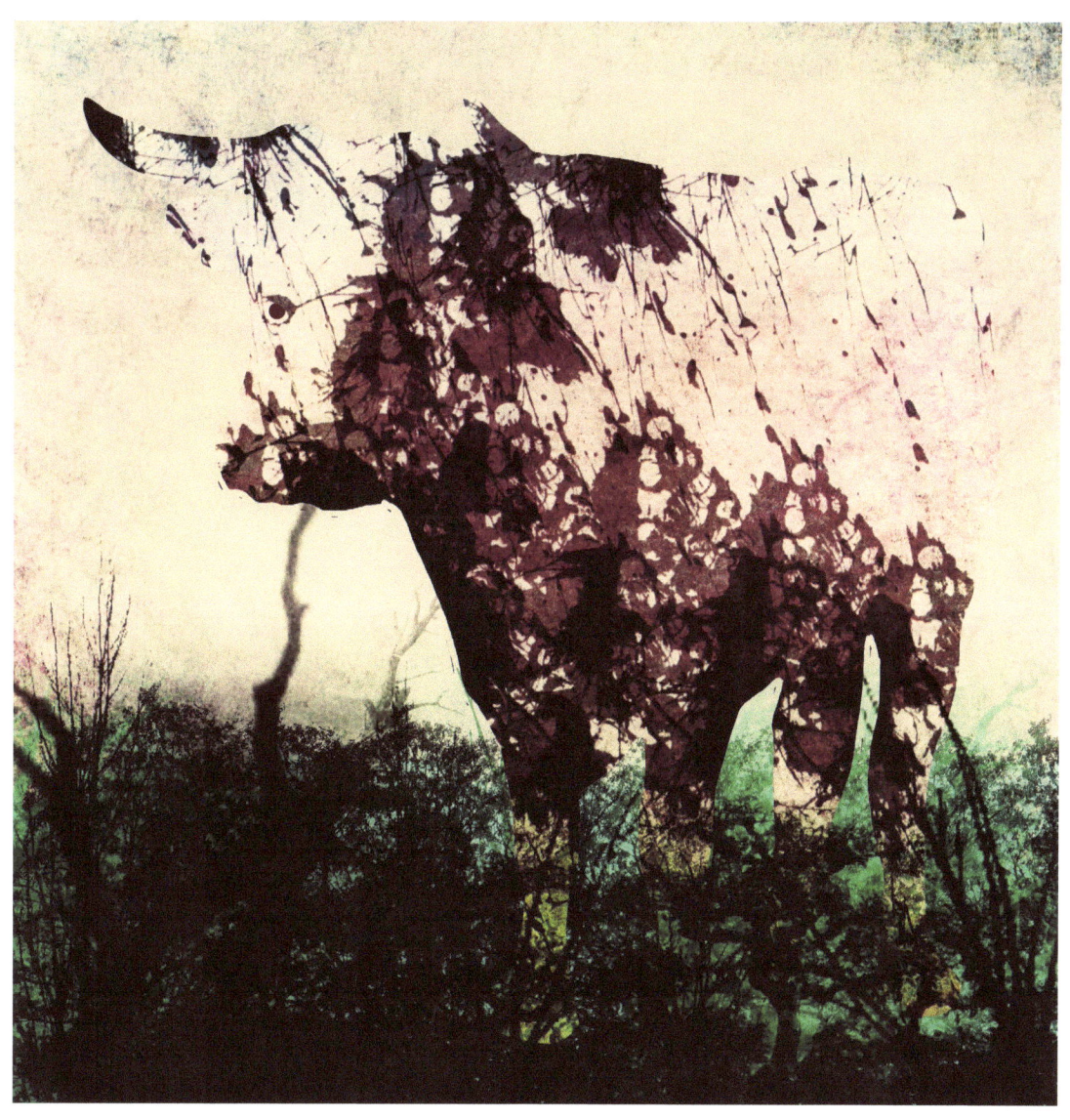

Bull in Grass

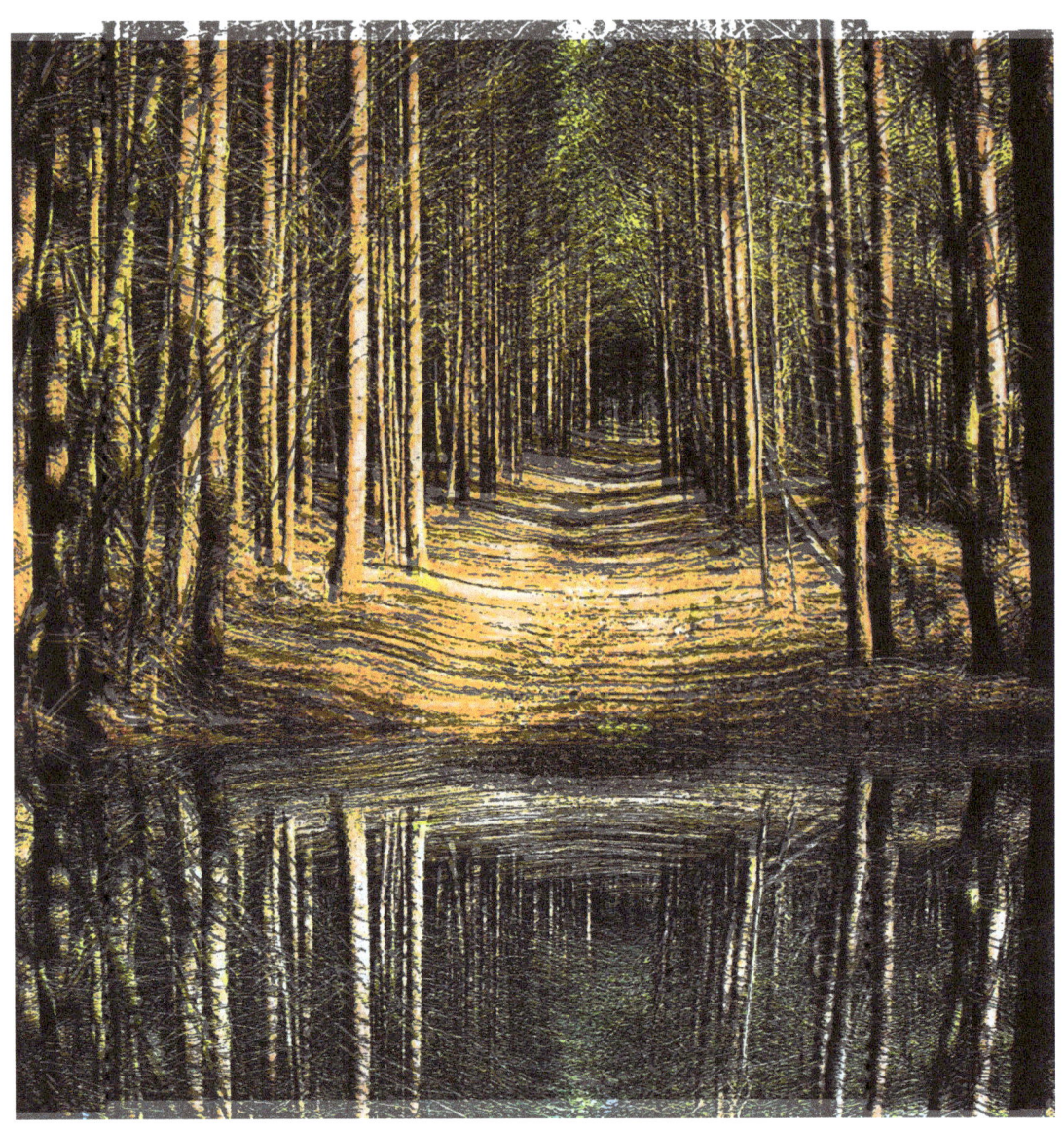

Cambria Forest

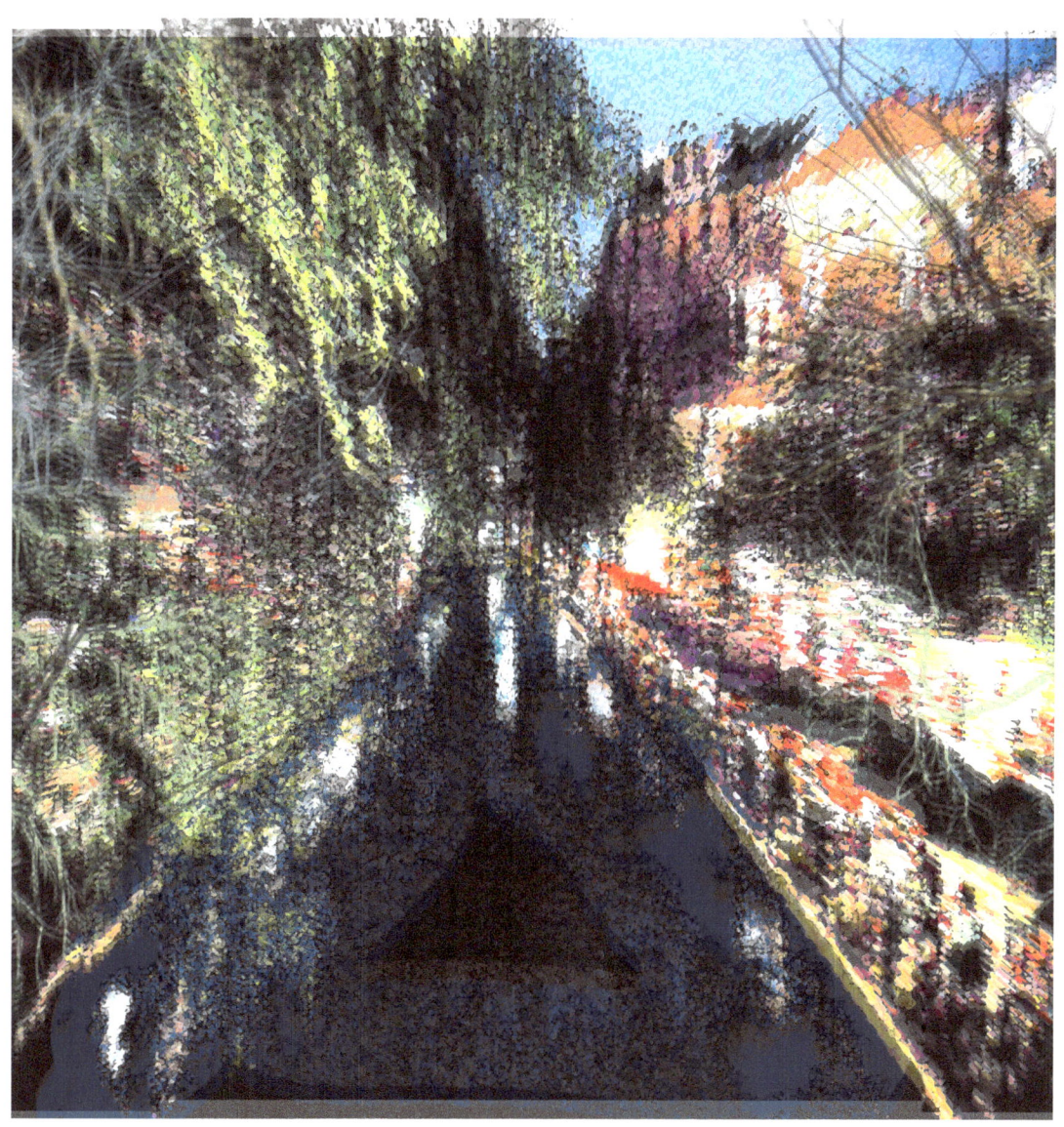

Canal Bistro

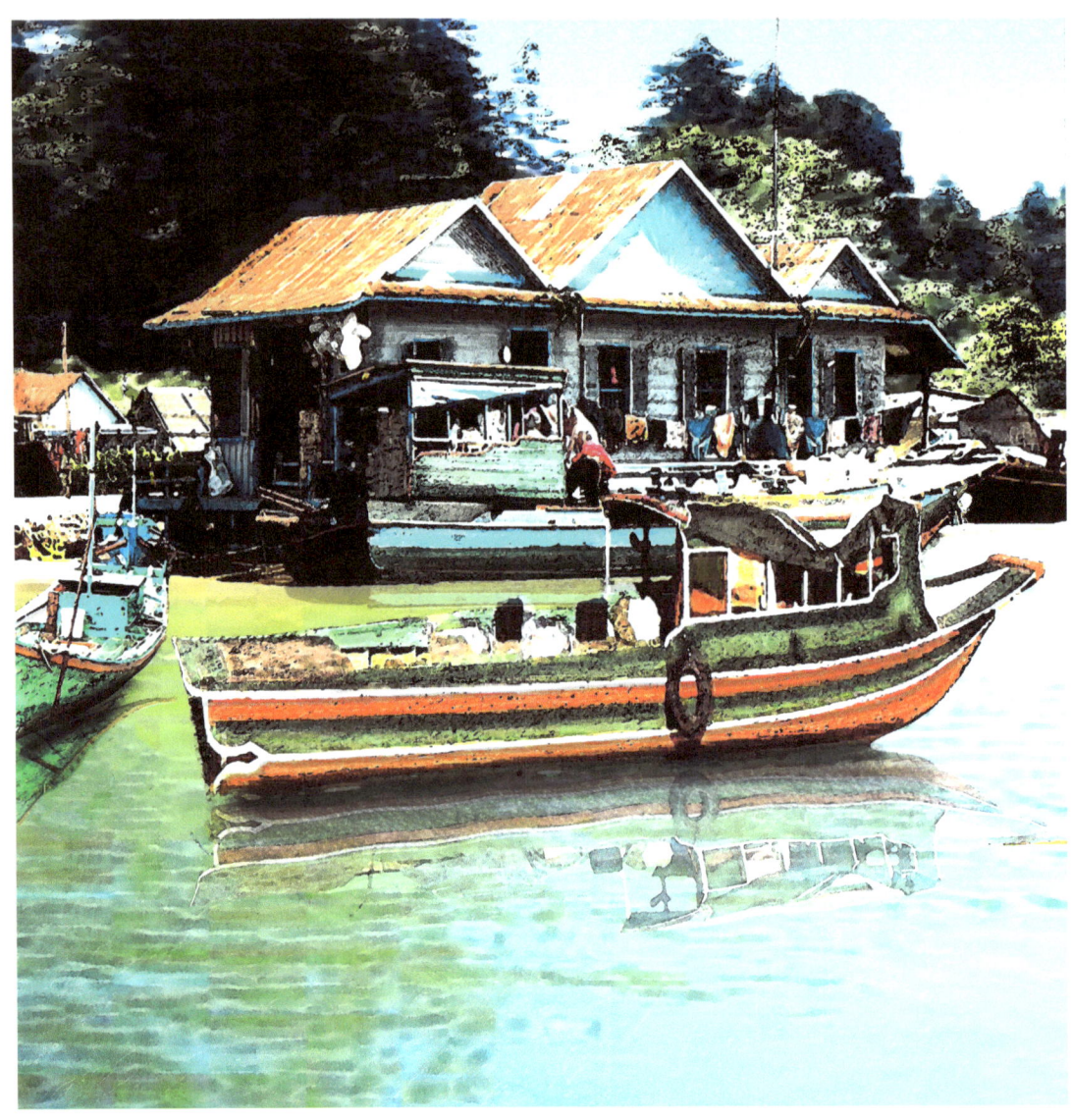

Catering Boat

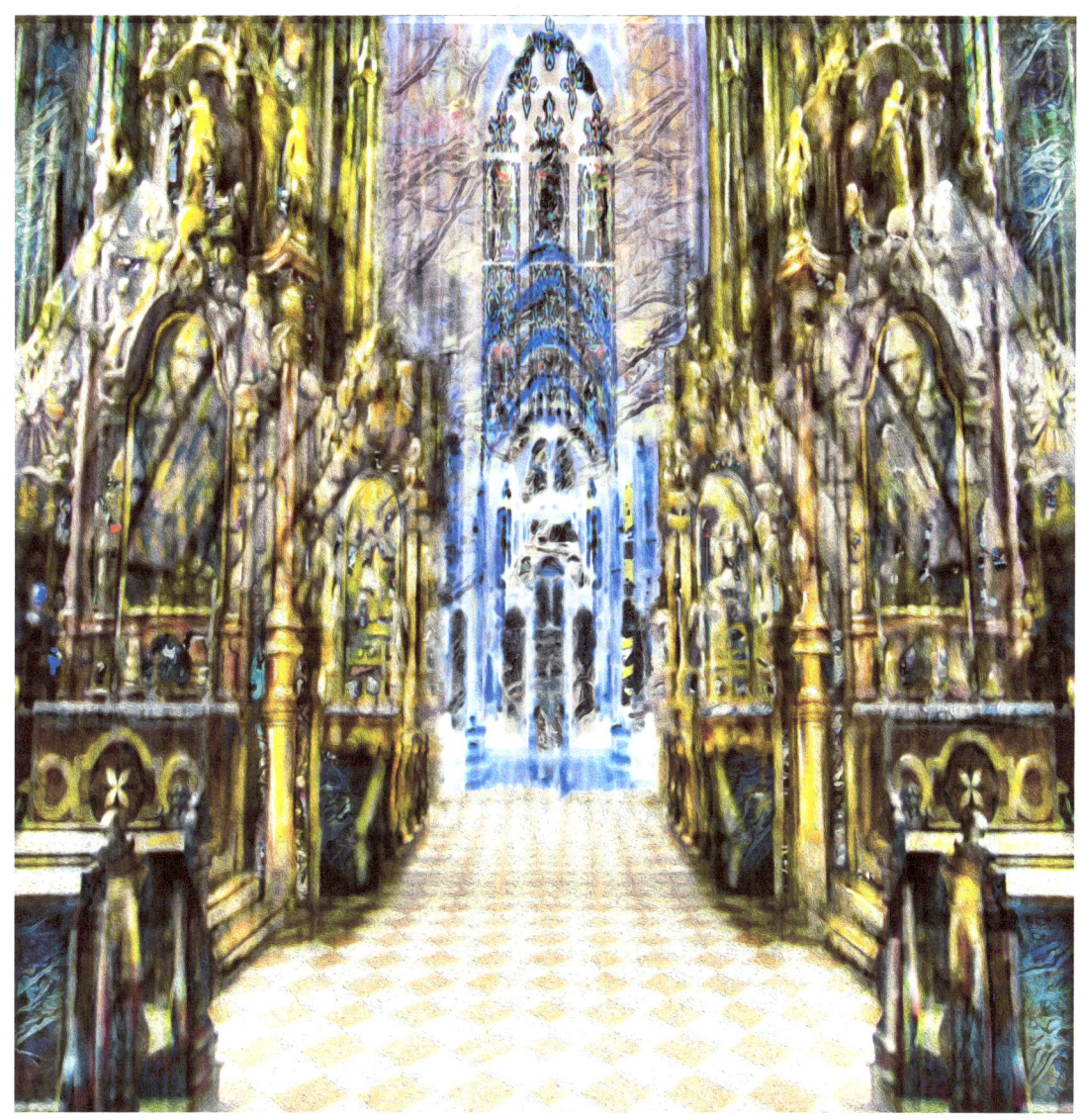

Cathedral

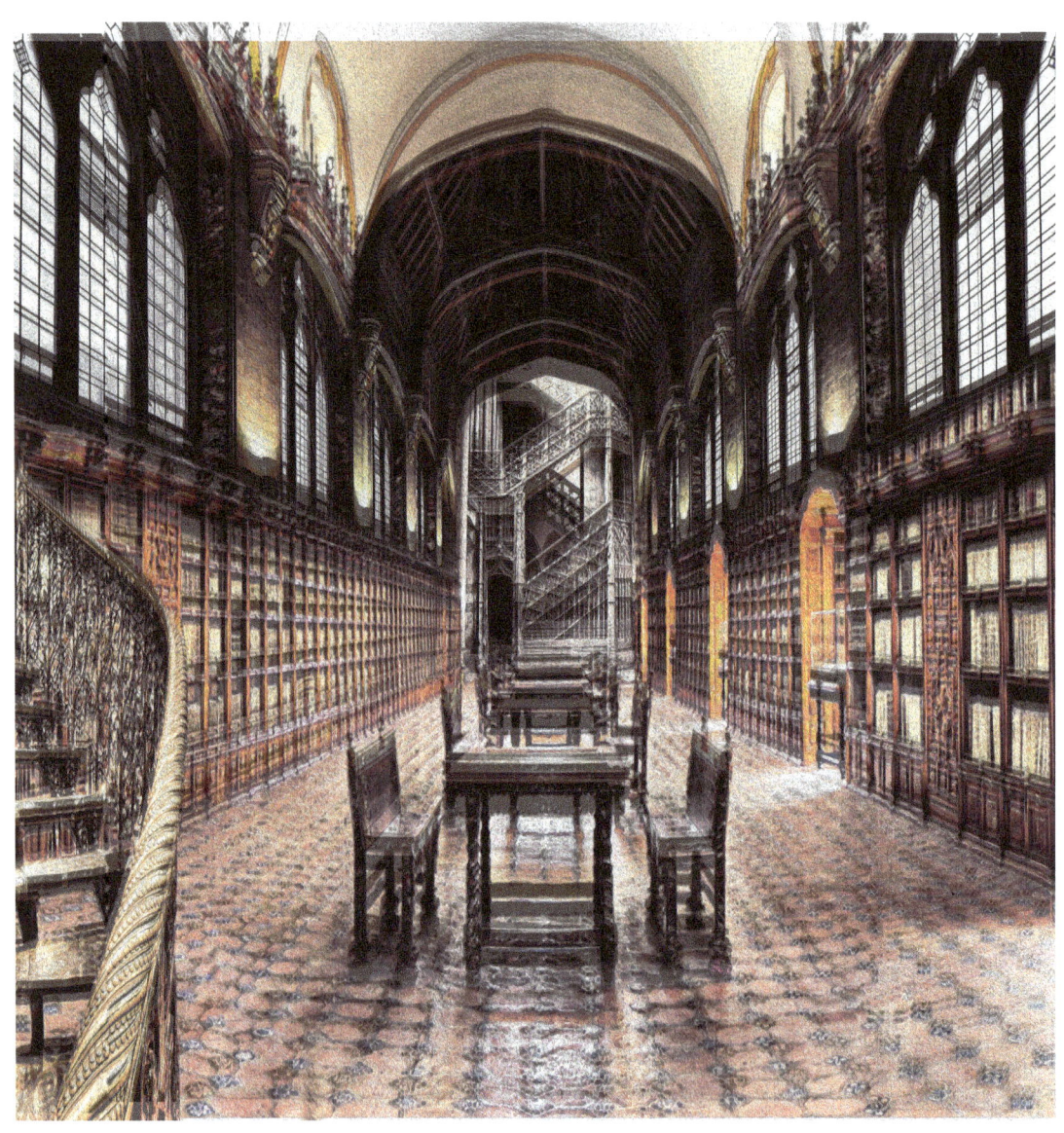

Cathedral Stairs

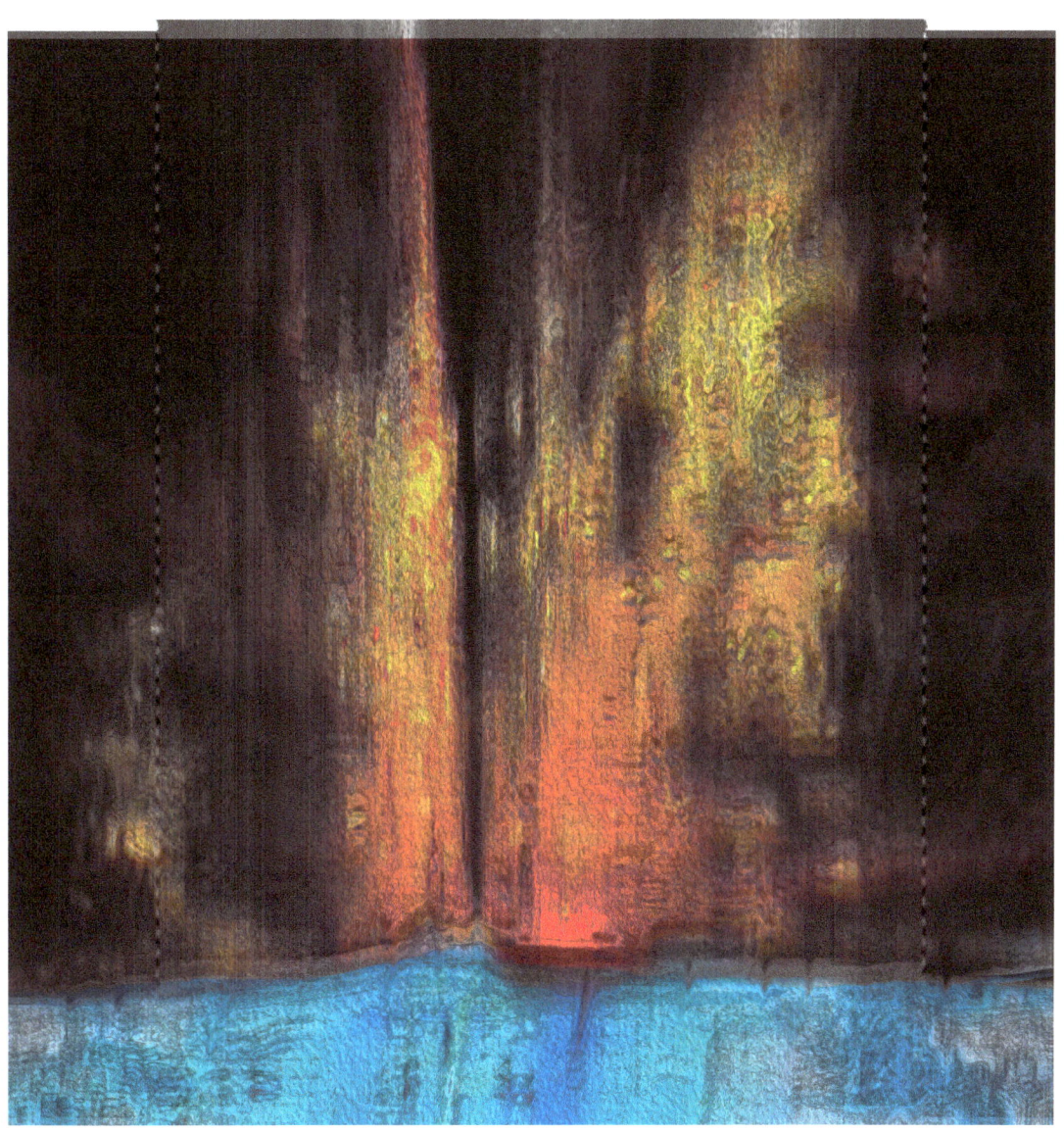

Cave Depth

About the Author

Dr. P. is a cognitive psychologist, writer, and artist. His research involves the reticular activating system and cognitive dissonance arousal. His paintings are known for stimulating incongruity to maximize thought provoking insights and new experiences. Welcome to his mind. Please also consider his newest paperback book releases

Surreal Art Reflections, Vol 3, ISBN 9781798140802

Surreal Art Reflections, Vol 2, ISBN 9781797970417

Facial Art Reflections ISBN 9781797751108
Abstract facial paintings.

How to Become an Alpha Being ISBN 9781797747774
Self-Help psychology for men and women.

Dante's Children's Colorbook ISBN 9781797754307
Color book of animals for children and adults alike.

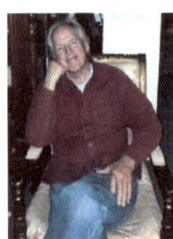

www.ingramcontent.com/pod-product-compliance
Lightning Source LLC
Chambersburg PA
CBHW051953210526
45473CB00024B/2082